BFI Film Classics

The BFI Film Classics series introduces, interprets and celebrates landmarks of world cinema. Each volume offers an argument for the film's 'classic' status, together with discussion of its production and reception history, its place within a genre or national cinema, an account of its technical and aesthetic importance, and in many cases, the author's personal response to the film.

For a full list of titles in the series, please visit https://www.bloomsbury.com/uk/series/bfi-film-classics/

La Jetée

Chris Darke

BFI

THE BRITISH FILM INSTITUTE
Bloomsbury Publishing Plc, 50 Bedford Square, London, WC1B 3DP, UK
Bloomsbury Publishing Inc, 1359 Broadway, New York, NY 10018, USA
Bloomsbury Publishing Ireland, 29 Earlsfort Terrace, Dublin 2, D02 AY28, Ireland

BLOOMSBURY is a trademark of Bloomsbury Publishing Plc

First published in 2016 by Palgrave on behalf of the British Film Institute
This edition first published in Great Britain 2026 by Bloomsbury on behalf of the British Film Institute, 21 Stephen Street, London, W1T 1LN
www.bfi.org.uk

The BFI is a cultural charity, a National Lottery distributor, and the UK's lead organisation for film and the moving image. We believe society needs stories. Film, television and the moving image bring them to life, helping us to connect and understand each other better. We share the stories of yesterday, search for the stories of today, and shape the stories of tomorrow.

Cover artwork: © Hokyoung Kim
Series cover design: Louise Dugdale
Series text design: Ketchup/SE14
Images from *La Jetée* (Chris Marker, 1963), © Argos Films (used with permission); *Staring Back* (1952–2006), courtesy the Chris Marker Estate and Peter Blum Gallery, New York; *Le Joli mai* (Chris Marker, 1962), Sofracinema; *Cléo de 5 à 7* (Agnès Varda, 1962), Rome–Paris Films; *Vertigo* (Alfred Hitchcock, 1958), © Alfred J. Hitchcock Productions
Additional image credits are listed on p. 93

A catalogue record for this book is available from the British Library.

A catalog record for this book is available from the Library of Congress.

ISBN: PB: 978-1-8390-2271-5
ePDF: 978-1-8390-2268-5
ePUB: 978-1-8390-2270-8

Printed and bound in India

For product safety related questions contact productsafety@bloomsbury.com.

To find out more about our authors and books visit www.bloomsbury.com and sign up for our newsletters.

Contents

Acknowledgments

My experience of writing this book was greatly enlivened by the Whitechapel Gallery's invitation to co-curate the exhibition *Chris Marker: A Grin Without a Cat* in 2014, the first UK retrospective show of the full range of Marker's work. Many thanks to the other curators involved: Magnus af Petersens, Christine Van Assche, Habda Rashid and Gareth Evans. Florence Dauman at Argos Films was immensely helpful in providing material for the show and granting access to the Argos archives, as well as in negotiating rights issues. Sophie Lewis and Trista Selous translated Marker's writing impeccably for the catalogue, and I remain indebted to them.

At the Cinémathèque royale de Belgique, Jean-Paul Dorchain allowed me to consult rare materials relating to *La Jetée*, and Nicola Mazzanti, director of the Cinémathèque, kindly let us exhibit them. I also thank those who assisted me at the BFI Reuben Library, the Bibliothèque du film at the Cinémathèque Française, and the Bibliothèque nationale de France. Warm salutations to Agnès Varda for her hospitality, John Burgan for letting me quote from his correspondence with Marker, and Thomas Tode for sharing the transcript of his interview with Alain Resnais. Thanks also to those who provided encouragement and support: Raymond Bellour, Richard Bevan, Tamsin Clark, Jem Cohen, Bill Horrigan, Emiko Omori, Daniel Potter, Libby Saxton, Isabel Stevens and Michael Witt. Thanks to Dominique Cabrera and Edmée Doroszlaï at Ad Libitum.

I particularly want to thank my editors at BFI Publishing/ Palgrave, Rebecca Barden, Nicola Cattini, Sophie Contento, Lucinda Knight and Jenna Steventon, for commissioning this book and their patience in seeing it through to completion. Many thanks to the Department of Media, Culture and Language at Roehampton University for supporting my research in Brussels and Paris.

Quotations from Marker's writing are reproduced by kind permission of the Estate of Christian Bouche-Villeneuve, known as Chris Marker: Pierre Nicolaÿ, Nicole Ezanno, Ghislaine Faure-Raynfeld, François Faure, Hugues Faure, Jean-Christian Faure, Raymonde Bouche and Mabel Nicolaÿ Duflo. Installation views of the *Chris Marker: A Grin Without a Cat* exhibition held at Whitechapel Gallery, London, 16 April–22 June 2014, courtesy of the Whitechapel Gallery Archive (photographs by Patrick Lears). Images from the *Staring Back* photographic series (1952–2006) are reproduced by kind permission of the Marker Estate and the Peter Blum Gallery, New York.

He had entered Death's kingdom without any markings, with no identity disc, no memory; she might pass him by, even touch him, without recognising him.

Chris Marker, *Le Coeur net* (1949)

1 *La Jetée* … Still

I don't remember when I first saw *La Jetée* (1963) or where. It might have been in a repertory fleapit or a university seminar room. Or did I discover it, this mysterious jewel of a film, dumped on a VHS tape among half-recorded TV shows and out-of-date ads? Imagine: tumbling on fast-forward through colourful junk when, suddenly, *this*. Press play. Monochrome images – cool, spare, static – which seem to unfold out of each other. Whispering. Sudden heart-swelling gusts of music. Then – did that just happen? How? Rewind. Watch again. Wait for *that* moment when the film itself looks straight back at you.

The 'where' and 'when' don't really matter now. The film has been a part of my life for so long that it seems always to have been there and over the years it has acquired the status of a work apart, and not only for me. When asked to contribute to the decennial *Sight and Sound* poll of the 'Greatest Films of All Time' in 2012, I had no trouble deciding which title would occupy prime position in my list and, in its first appearance, *La Jetée* came in at number fifty out of a hundred films, tying with Mizoguchi's *Ugetsu monogatari* (1953) – curiously, another film about ghosts and wartime – but was kept from the top slot by Hitchcock's 'pre-make', *Vertigo* (1958). If such polls amount to anything, then *La Jetée* can no longer be considered merely a 'cult classic', as it has often been called, and should now be recognised as a bona fide master-work, a classic fully fledged and with no need of qualification.

Not that there isn't something eminently cult-like about the admiration it inspires, the best expression of which must be the tiny one-room bar named in its honour in the Shinjuku district of Tokyo, where people come to drink beneath images from the film and which Marker stated was worth more to him than 'any number of Oscars'.[1] Other tributes are better known: from Terry Gilliam's 1995 Hollywood 'remake' *Twelve Monkeys* and Mark Romanek's video for David Bowie's 1993 single 'Jump They Say', to the many science-fiction films that have drawn on *La Jetée*'s spiralling time-travel narrative, among them the *Back to the Future* series (1985–90) and the *Terminator* films (1984–) as well as *Primer* (2004) and *Looper* (2012), not to mention the US television series *12 Monkeys* (2015–18) (which, if we accept Marker's claim that *La Jetée* was itself a remake of *Vertigo*, makes the TV series a remake of a remake of a ...).

In a well-known essay on cult films, Umberto Eco distinguishes between 'unhinged' and 'perfect' works. The 'unhinged' film is easily reduced to quotable fragments ripe for semiotic recycling and cult appreciation. The 'perfect' film, on the other hand, resists such intertextual overhauling because it remains in our minds as a whole, 'in the form of a central idea or emotion'.[2] But what about films that are both 'unhinged' *and* 'perfect', emotionally and intellectually complete as well as seemingly easy to disassemble? *La Jetée* is just such a work. 'Unhinged' in its highly unconventional and already fragmented form, it is also peculiarly 'perfect' for the same reason. I'd go further. *La Jetée* is perfect enough in its unhinged-ness to be exhibited in a gallery.

It is one thing to write a book about *La Jetée*, quite another to dedicate a room to it (and not a bar this time). The room in question was at the Whitechapel Gallery in London where an exhibition of Marker's work was on show and I found myself returning to it repeatedly between April and June 2014. The challenge of how best to fit a black box into a white cube, of reconciling the viewing conditions of cinema with those of a gallery, found an answer in the room's layout. Rows of benches facing a screen approximated the experience of being at the movies. The lighting levels, dimmed but not quite dark, and the space left for people to circulate around one side of the seating, allowed gallery-goers to pause, watch for a moment and then move on. I realised I could do something in that room I'd

Watching the watchers (installation view of *Chris Marker: A Grin Without a Cat*, exhibition held at Whitechapel Gallery, 16 April–22 June 2014. Courtesy Whitechapel Gallery, Whitechapel Gallery Archive)

never done before, something that wouldn't normally be possible among the darkened rows of a cinema or the brightly lit distractions of home viewing. I could watch people watching *La Jetée*.

Whether I was standing at the entrance or sitting on the benches alongside other viewers, my attention invariably shifted away from the film to the audience. And while there was something slightly recursive to the act of watching people watch a film about a man who watches the mental images projected in his mind's eye, what did I see in those faces? Rapt attention, no doubt, and the signs of moment-by-moment immersion in the unique experience that the film offers. If my avid observation of the audience sounds a bit odd, I should explain that, as one of the curators of the show, I was bound to be intrigued by the way people reacted. Walking through the other two rooms, among the photographs and multimedia installations, books and collages, I was impressed by the absorbed looks of the visitors. Each room also included a looped projection of a film shown in its entirety: in the first, Marker's early collaboration with Alain Resnais, *Les Statues meurent aussi* (*Statues Also Die*, 1953), and in the third, a restored print of *Le Fond de l'air est rouge*

(*A Grin Without a Cat*, 1977), Marker's three-and-a-half-hour documentary fresco about the leftist movements of the 1960s.

But it was in the room between the other two where I did most of my audience-watching. Though the smallest by far, it provided a focus to the show, being the only room dedicated solely to a single film. A little under thirty minutes long, shot in black and white, made up almost entirely of still images and with an evocative combination of voiceover narration, sound effects and music, *La Jetée* is cinematically hard to classify; something alluded to in the title credits where it is described as 'un photo-roman', or 'a photo-novel'. With haunting economy, it tells the story of a soldier (Davos Hanich), who is held captive in an underground prison camp in post-apocalypse Paris and used as a guinea pig in time-travel experiments. He retains a mental image from his childhood of the face of a woman (Hélène Chatelain) and the death of a man witnessed on the observation pier ('la jetée') of Orly airport in Paris. His captors exploit the strength of this image, first to send him back to the past, where he meets the woman again, then into the future to secure the fate of humanity's survivors. His mission accomplished, the time traveller flees back in time to Orly, where he hopes to be reunited with the woman, but he has been pursued by a guard from the camp who executes him in front of her. The time traveller's final realisation is that his childhood image was of his own death.

Even though it was made over sixty years ago, *La Jetée* seems to have escaped the ravages of time, which explains something of its enduring fascination. Film-makers have played extensive variations on its story; artists have lingered over its exploration of the photographic image; and critics have analysed it as a meditation on loss, memory and the nature of cinema. However, in curating the Whitechapel show we found proof that *La Jetée* did not, in fact, fall fully formed from the sky as an inimitable cinematic masterpiece, but that it had its phases of production, its first drafts and rough sketches and even, as we discovered, its 'twin'. To unearth such material was significant for two reasons. First, because Marker was deeply averse to giving interviews and rarely spoke about his work, next to nothing is known about the film's origins or the ideas behind it. Such reticence adds greatly to its enduring mystique as a work that speaks for itself and as a seeming anomaly, the only fiction film in Marker's extensive cinematic oeuvre. Second, because there is almost nothing in Marker's own words, the material we assembled afforded a rare insight into the work that went into shaping the film.

I had read in an essay by the film scholar Philippe Dubois that the Royal Film Archive of Belgium holds a trove of material relating to *La Jetée*, including a copy of a different version of the film, an exercise book containing an editing plan and a collection of correspondence between Marker and Jacques Ledoux, the former director of the Film Archive. Ledoux had assisted Marker with his research for *La Jetée* by arranging screenings of science-fiction films for him, and Marker had in turn donated materials to the Archive, as well as giving his friend an enigmatic credit on the film for the so-called 'Ledoux Process' ('Procédé Ledoux') and casting him in the role of the Chief Experimenter. So, in April 2013 I travelled to Brussels where, in the Archive's gabled library, I examined these items with a sense of anticipation that was only heightened by the discovery that the Marker–Ledoux correspondence had mysteriously

Jacques Ledoux as Chief Experimenter

gone missing. (Dubois treats his readers to some extracts. Marker to Ledoux in early 1962: 'a role as experimental-doctor-in-a-World-War-Three-underground-concentration-camp awaits you, which will fit you like a glove').[3] The copy of the film held by the Archive – *La Jetée*'s 'twin' – was distinguished from its definitive sibling by only the slightest difference in appearance; but when it comes to stillness and movement a difference, however small, can be decisive. What was striking was how and where Marker had chosen *not* to tell the story in still images. In this version, the opening pre-credits sequence set on the main pier at Orly airport is filmed in motion. The camera pans from left to right in a high-angle shot following the time traveller as he runs towards the woman, the image of whose face haunts him, and so towards the death which, through some quirk of time, he will have seen – and foreseen – as a child. This moving shot lasts only ten seconds but it alters the balance of the film completely.

If this version of the film raised questions about the beginning (and beginnings) of *La Jetée*, the other archival item I had to examine took me even further back in time to its prehistory. Slipping on a pair of white gloves, I opened a large manila envelope and extracted a spiral-bound A4 exercise book with a blue cover and the word 'Sciences' embossed in gold. Turning to the inside front page, I saw the film's title scrawled in thick strokes. The handwriting was familiar. Marker had made his mark with the pen he took his pen name from. Over the following twenty-eight pages the structure of the film is arranged in a series of fourteen sequences listed alphabetically from A to Q. Each sequence is laid out across facing pages, with the left-hand page containing images and the right handwritten (though not by Marker) editing instructions. (The exceptions being sequences B, J and K, which are missing from the document but acknowledged in the overall alphabetical sequence.) The images had been cut from contact sheets, pasted vertically onto the page, and each one numbered, their order relating to an early version of the film's narrative sequence. This 'workbook', as we curators came to call it, was like a secret manual of the film, a unique

The workbook title page

and fragile assembly (some images falling ungummed from its pages) of the elements that make up the completed work. Particularly interesting is the comparative exchange it sets up with the film, for there are things in the workbook that are not in the film and things in the film that are not in the workbook.

These two archival treasures, *La Jetée*'s 'twin' and the workbook, were the principal displays in the Whitechapel room dedicated to the film. The Archive's print was only available in the French-language version, with Jean Négroni's narration translated in English subtitles, and it happened to be the most luminous copy of the film I'd ever seen. Probably because it had rarely, if ever, been projected as a celluloid print, the high-definition digital transfer was pristine, with monochrome tones that glowed like silk. From the workbook, we had facsimiles made of the title page and six sequences (A, M, N, O, P and Q) selected to illustrate either how close they are to the final version of the film or how they differ from it. In an adjoining vitrine, two other printed versions of the film's images and text were shown, one published in 1964 by the French magazine *L'Avant-Scène Cinéma*, the other being the 1992 hardback 'ciné-roman' designed by Bruce Mau.

One day, as we arranged the pages with our white gloves, preparing them for their vitrines, I said to a colleague, 'We're going to be accused of being fetishists.' (Fetishism: the act of sanctifying fragments. See Eco's definition of 'cult'.) And with good reason.

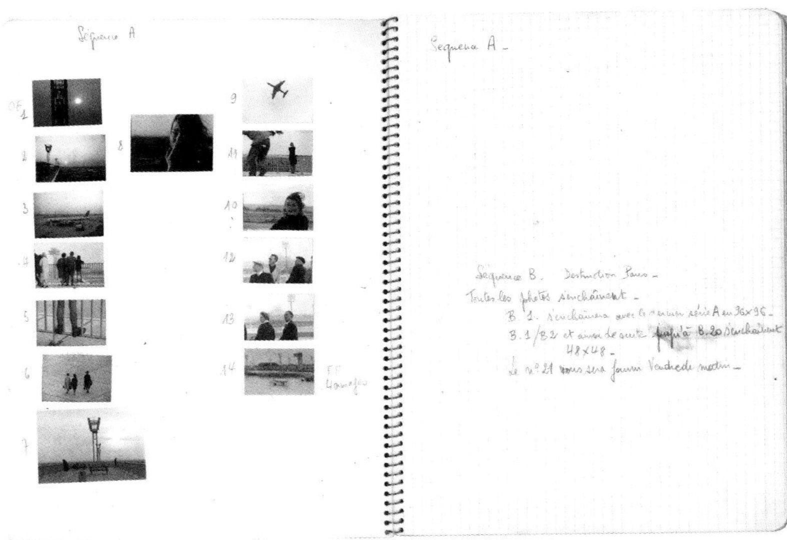

The workbook: vitrine display (installation view of *Chris Marker: A Grin Without a Cat*, exhibition held at Whitechapel Gallery, 16 April–22 June 2014. Courtesy Whitechapel Gallery, Whitechapel Gallery Archive); layout for Sequence A

Two good reasons, in fact, the first being strictly curatorial. These different paper versions of the film – workbook, magazine layout and ciné-roman – together proposed a way of taking seriously its description as a 'photo-roman', but they also represented an aspect of the way Marker worked. He described himself as a '*bricoleur*', or a 'tinkerer', extracting material from diverse sources to recombine it anew in a different medium, whether as a book, film, CD-ROM or some subsequent digital iteration, often reconfiguring that medium in the process. With Marker we move constantly from word to image, page to screen, book to film and back again, sometimes even in the same work. Images are rarely without their accompanying text or spoken commentary. The screen has the attributes of a page, and the page those of a screen. A book's a film and a film's a book. If an attention to detail bordering on the fetishistic is needed to even begin to unbraid the dense weave of media, materials and elements that makes up Marker's work, then so be it.

The other reason for my trepidation was more personal. A phrase kept coming back to me during the preparations for the show. It was something I'd read on another research trip, this time to the archives of Argos Films, the French production company founded by Anatole Dauman in 1951, which had produced many of Marker's films, including *La Jetée*. The phrase appeared in a letter where Marker took Dauman to task for talking about him publicly at a televised awards ceremony. 'Every homage is a disguised act of aggression', he rebuked his long-suffering producer.[4] When Marker died in July 2012, aged ninety-one, the reaction was extraordinary given the low profile he had guarded for years. News of his death trended on Twitter second only to the Olympics. Street art tributes appeared on Paris walls. A makeshift public shrine manifested on a Brooklyn sidewalk. In London and New York, memorial screening programmes stretched late into the night. Major gallery shows followed in quick succession: at the Centre Pompidou in Paris, at the Massachusetts Institute of Technology's Visual Arts Centre and at the Whitechapel in London.[5] If these were acts of aggression, they came well disguised as expressions of respect and affection, of something little short of love. But I couldn't help thinking that behind this posthumous outpouring there was some truth to Marker's uncompromising, and uncharacteristically Freudian, formula. For if it was only after his death that it became possible to start to get to grips with the full extent of his achievements, this required that his work be approached in ways he had actively resisted when alive, that's to say, with a certain degree of 'aggression'.

Take Marker's attitude towards his early films, for instance. When the Cinémathèque Française presented a retrospective of his films in 1998, which Marker curated himself, he stated, 'For a long time I've limited the choice of my films which have the good fortune to be programmed to those made after 1962, the year of *Le Joli mai* and *La Jetée*.'[6] He explained that this decision was motivated not by any 'retrospective self-censorship' of the films he'd made about Communist countries in the 1950s and early 1960s but by a wish to spare the public work that he now regarded as being little more than the 'rudimentary sketches' of an 'apprentice'.[7] This facet of Marker as his own curator is part of his identity as an experimental artist who remained focused on the future by reappraising elements of his past work. In terms of his cinematic back catalogue, this approach saw later films displacing earlier ones if their treatment of subject matter was deemed to be more fully achieved. So *Le Fond de l'air est rouge* superseded *¡Cuba Sí!* (1961) in its analysis of communism; *Sans soleil* (*Sunless*, 1983) replaced *Le Mystère Koumiko* (*The Koumiko Mystery*, 1965) as a portrait of Japan; and *Le Tombeau d'Alexandre* (*The Last Bolshevik*, 1993) absorbed *Le Train en marche* (*The Train Rolls On*, 1971) as a study of Soviet-era film-maker Aleksandr Medvedkin. In his later, post-filmic period, this curatorial principle can also be seen at work in the encyclopaedic *bricolage* of the CD-ROM *Immemory* (1998), as well as in the *Ouvroir* (2008), Marker's own imaginary museum in the virtual world of Second Life. In *La Jetée*, too, pre-existing fragments of his work are repurposed to new ends.

As curators, we wanted to display Marker's work in all its forms, to be able to give British audiences their first opportunity to explore its diversity and internal coherence. To do the job properly meant defying his lifetime wishes about which of his films he wanted shown, especially when two of his pre-1962 titles, *Dimanche à Pékin* (*Sunday in Peking*, 1956) and *Lettre de Sibérie* (*Letter from Siberia*, 1958), were re-released following his death in newly restored versions. No question, then, that our homage was anything other than an accumulation of 'aggressions'. We unearthed, translated and republished some of his early writing in the catalogue for the show. And as for the material in the room dedicated to *La Jetée*, it was inconceivable that he would have consented to these 'sketches' being shown when he was alive. While I was confident that they would in no way detract from the finished film and only add to our understanding of it, the curatorial dilemma of whether or not to show particular works was sharpened for me by the fact that I had come to know Marker personally in the last thirteen years of his life.[8]

As the years go by and time does its work, I think of my encounters with him as though with a character passed into a legend of his own making. In his way, Marker was as self-mythologising as Orson Welles, but he was the anti-Welles in how he went about constructing his legend – where 'legend' means both 'fabled character' and 'cover-story' – and by withdrawing behind one the other emerged in his absence, encouraged by the mingling of fact and rumour. He had served in the French Resistance and American Army in World War II (true). He refused to be photographed (mostly true). He was, in fact, a Martian (unconfirmed). Marker's lifelong campaign of self-concealment required multiple aliases: Sergei Murasaka, Sandor Krasna, Michel Krasna, Hayao Yamaneko, Fritz Markassin, T. T. Toukanov, Jacopo Berenizi, Boris Villeneuve, Marc Dornier, Chris Mayor and Chris. Marker. 'Chris Marker' (minus the abbreviating dot) was only the most well-known pseudonym behind which the man born Christian François Bouche-Villeneuve in 1921 chose to operate. Later in life, perhaps as a caution to his

Alexandra Stewart, Ligia Branice, William and Janine Klein from the *Staring Back* photographic series (1952–2006, courtesy the Chris Marker Estate and Peter Blum Gallery, New York) …

… and *La Jetée* (1963)

followers not to take such self-concealment too seriously, he engaged with the world through the intermediary of an orange-and-black-striped cartoon cat called Guillaume-en-Égypte. Marker took this preference for discretion, fostered by a habit of wartime clandestinity and compounded by an ideological aversion to self-promotion, to the point where it became a working method, but one in which the work was productively shared with his followers. Marker leaves it up to us to make the connections, to join the dots and do the detective work, thereby becoming co-authors in the author's absence.

It was in this spirit that we invited visitors to make sense of the photographs in the room, selected from Marker's 2007 photographic series *Staring Back*, which drew on images he had taken throughout his life. In a radio interview given shortly after Marker's death, Hélène Chatelain described the group that worked on *La Jetée* as 'a real cabal of friends', some of whom were represented in the photographs.[9] Among them was Alexandra Stewart, the Canadian-born actress who features as 'a face of happiness' in *La Jetée* and who reads the English-language commentary in *Sans soleil*. Also on the walls were images of Ligia Branice, actress-wife of film-maker Walerian Borowczyk, who plays one of the 'people of the future', among whom the American photographer William Klein and his wife Janine also appear, photographed on the set for the film. Chatelain is a film-maker, writer and translator, and well qualified to discuss Marker's work. In her radio interview she observed that Marker had 'a relationship with images as a sort of echo. Normally an echo disappears but these don't. And when an echo doesn't disappear it can effectively become a character. That's a completely literary approach.'[10] It is an idea I will draw on in this book which, in many respects, comes out of that room.

2 In the Beginning

In 1962, the year he filmed *Le Joli mai* and started work on *La Jetée*, Marker had turned forty-one and was already an established writer and film-maker. His first post-war appearance in print was in 1946, and over the next decade he would be a prolific author of reviews, essays, poems and stories, published mostly in the left-leaning Catholic monthly *Esprit*. At the same time, he was working for *Esprit*'s publisher Éditions du Seuil as a commissioning editor, book designer and translator of English-language titles. Seuil also published nine books by him, including two lavishly illustrated volumes of film commentaries (1961 and 1967), a critical essay on the writer Jean Giraudoux (1951) and his only novel, *Le Coeur net* (*The Forthright Spirit*, 1949), elements of which would inform the story of *La Jetée*.

It's worth stressing this conjunction of writing and film-making in Marker's creative development. Although it's correct to say that he started out as a writer and subsequently turned to cinema, this implies that one activity replaced, or superseded, the other but, as he began to write more for the screen than the page, it was precisely his skill as a literary stylist that distinguished his approach to cinema. So much so that other film-makers called on him as a commentary-writer – of the ten short to medium-length films that Marker collaborated on between 1952 and 1962 he wrote the commentaries for seven – and critics decided that a new category was needed to describe his work. Borrowing Jean Vigo's formulation of his own film *À propos de Nice* (1930) as presenting a 'documentary point of view', André Bazin defined *Lettre de Sibérie* as an '"essay", understood in the same sense that it has in literature – an essay at once historical and political, written by a poet as well'.[11]

The six films Marker had made by 1962 established a unique voice in post-war French cinema, 'a 1 to 1.33 Montaigne', as Richard

Roud put it.[12] Marker took full advantage of the freedom the essay allows for the writer's voice to slalom through different registers: to be grave one moment and playful the next; to set personal impressions against political analysis; to make lists, take notes and observe the flora and fauna, as though composing a letter to a friend conveying the wonders and woes of the corners of the world from which he was writing. In this sense, Marker's commentaries – 'fascinating, maddening, highly literary … (Malraux plus Giraudoux divided by *x*)' – merit the term 'essay'.[13] And the term would stick, perhaps even becoming too prescriptive over time and serving eventually to corral the bewildering variety of Marker's cinema into the generic paddock of the 'essay film'. For if there was ever a film-maker whose work seems designed to resist established categories, it was Marker; to call *La Jetée* a 'photo-roman', for instance, is surely a joke on the classificatory urge itself.

Whether he was writing, taking photographs or making films – or writing *and* taking photographs *and* making films – these activities reflected his overarching passion for seeing the world. Marker travelled widely and his early filmography reads like so many stamps in a globetrotter's passport: Helsinki for the 1952 Olympic Games in *Olympia 52* (1952); Mao-era China for *Dimanche à Pékin*; the USSR for *Lettre de Sibérie*; the young state of Israel for *Description d'un combat* (*Description of a Struggle*, 1960); and post-revolutionary Cuba for *¡Cuba Sí!*.

With a decade's worth of film-making behind him by 1962, Marker proceeded to challenge the presiding expectations of his work. After years of travelling, he would make his next two films in his home city of Paris and, following the publication of the first volume of his *Commentaires* in 1961 – by which time he must have been wearily familiar with the pun 'Comment-taire?' ('How to shut up?') – *Le Joli mai* and *La Jetée* each signalled a stylistic departure from the essay film. *Le Joli mai* was an experiment in 'direct cinema', the latest innovation in documentary film-making, which enabled a small crew to film with unprecedented flexibility thanks to developments in lightweight camera and portable sound-recording technology. The resulting two-and-a-half-hour portrait of Paris, so deftly shot by Pierre Lhomme that he was given a co-director's credit, depended less on Marker's commentary and granted unusual prominence to vox pop interviews. With *La Jetée*, his first fiction film, Marker returned to the type of stories he'd written after World War II. And having journeyed far and wide in space, he would now travel in time.

The first thing to do with such a film, then, is to check its dates. In doing so we discover a small but not insignificant detail. The release date of *La Jetée* is usually given as 1962 but, in fact, this was the date when Marker signed the contract to make the film. Dated 19 February 1962, the contract specified that he was to make 'a short film of around twenty minutes during the course of 1962' for which the budget was 60,000 New Francs (roughly £8,000 in modern currency). Judging from the wording of the document, the film's genre had already been decided on, as had the unusual method by which it would be made. It was to be 'a science-fiction film shot as a frame-by-frame animation in black and white'.[14] Marker would work on *La Jetée* throughout 1962 and 1963 while also whittling down the fifty-plus hours of footage shot for *Le Joli mai*, which would itself be released in May 1963. After screenings at festivals in July and October 1963, *La Jetée* would receive its first public projection at the Cinéma La Pagode in Paris on 15 April 1964.

Almost forty years later, Marker recalled the production of *La Jetée* in a rare interview, conducted by email with the French newspaper *Libération*. 'It was made like a piece of automatic writing', he recollected:

> I was filming *Le Joli mai*, completely immersed in the reality of Paris 1962, and the euphoric discovery of 'direct cinema' (you will never make me say 'cinéma vérité') and on the crew's day off, I photographed a story I didn't completely understand. It was in the editing that the pieces of the puzzle came together, and it wasn't me who designed the puzzle. I'd have a hard time taking credit for it. It just happened, that's all.[15]

In fact, it had been some time happening. On several occasions in the late 1950s and early 1960s Marker alluded to projects anticipating *La Jetée* and pointed out the difficulties in realising them. In a 1957 interview, he mentioned his desire to make 'A medium or feature-length "science fiction" film'. Acknowledging that science fiction was not a genre common to French cinema (an extraordinary thought in the land of Jules Verne and Georges Méliès), he added, 'But I fear that the French aren't quite Martian enough.'[16] In 1962, he described wanting to make 'A futuristic film. But that costs too much and would hardly be possible.'[17] This obstacle at least would be overcome by the imaginative technical solution of using stills instead of moving images.

In February 1962, Anatole Dauman wrote to the French national public broadcaster Radiodiffusion-Télévision Française (RTF), proposing a 50/50 co-production deal between Argos Films and the Service de la Recherche at RTF, and a contract signed in May committed it to provide 33 per cent of the budget. The head of the Service de la Recherche was Pierre Schaeffer, a writer, composer, media theorist and, as inventor of *musique concrète*, a sonic pioneer. Schaeffer founded the unit in 1960 as an experimental audio-visual laboratory, and during the fifteen years of its existence it was involved in making over 700 films, including such far-out hybrids of animation and electro-acoustic music as René Laloux's feature-length box-office hit *La Planète Sauvage* (*Fantastic Planet*, 1973) and Jacques Rouxel's celebrated TV series *Les Shadoks* (1968–74) – think *The Clangers* (1969–74), but line-drawn, spikier and more anarchic. So *La Jetée*, as one of the Service de la Recherche's early ventures, can be fairly described as a TV co-production and a work of experimental animation.[18]

Schaeffer's outfit receives a special kind of acknowledgment in the opening credits. A little under thirty seconds into the film, the words 'Avec la participation du Service de la Recherche de la RTF' ('With the participation of the Service de la Recherche of RTF') appear and – for a blink-and-you'll-miss-it instant – '*Recherche*' is replaced by the word '*Trouvaille*'. At one level, this single-frame

'Searching' and 'finding' in the title sequence

word-flicker plays on 'searching' and 'finding', with *trouvaille* meaning 'a thing found by chance' or – and its fleeting appearance makes perfect sense here – 'a flash of inspiration'. But this little word of revelation, craftily hidden in the folds of a film that has barely begun, also carries a heavier freight of meaning and purpose.

One of the things it does is replace the opening shot in the other cut of the film. In comparing the two different openings, it's clear that Marker had not dispensed entirely with the idea of showing movement at the beginning of the film. If the purpose of the shot of Davos Hanich running along the airport pier in the alternative opening was to allude to the moment later on in the film when Hélène Chatelain opens her eyes, then that allusion is retained in the definitive opening but, instead of being demonstratively exhibited, it is condensed and suggested. First, by a camera movement that pulls back along the still image of the pier which, combined with the sound of the roar of a jet engine, makes it momentarily hard to tell what is moving and what is static. And second, by the '*Recherche*'-'*Trouvaille*' flashcut that follows this pull-back and foreshadows the *coup de cinéma* to come. Images of Chatelain opening her eyes are missing from the film's workbook, and the moment is instead referred to in a handwritten note as the '*séquence réveil*' ('awakening sequence') and in brackets with the word '*truqua*', an abbreviation of '*truquage*' ('special effect'). The '*trouvaille*' in the film's credits, then, is a subliminal signal of the '*truquage*' to come.

Trouvaille is also a word with a specific set of connotations in twentieth-century art, taking in André Breton's ideas about the Surrealist found object, Marcel Duchamp's 'readymades' and Max Ernst's 'found-interpreted objects'. This lineage pronounces art to be a thing of chance in which things themselves – everyday objects, images and words – are given the chance to become art. Marker was well aware of this. In his 1951 book on Jean Giraudoux, he wrote:

> Since the beginning of the century, through the conversation-poems of Apollinaire, the newspaper collages of Picasso and Braque and the tracings of Max Ernst, to Calder's mobiles and the tick tock shocks of McLaren via others that were less foreseen, a plot unfolds ... which consists of raising the most humble things from the disdain to which they were abandoned by the art of the egotistical, humanist and megalomaniacal periods. ... Redemption extends to the whole of creation; gold and lead are guests at the same supper (with a preference for lead).[19]

Marker the *bricoleur*, whose films incorporate all manner of material – illustrations, animations, photographs, printed ephemera, sequences from other films – places himself squarely in this tradition.

And if, as Chatelain suggests, images in his work have their own 'echoes', then one way of thinking about *La Jetée* is as a kind of echo-chamber for the *trouvailles* Marker found in his own archives and reframed in the film.

Argos Films promoted *La Jetée* as a groundbreaking experiment in form and genre in order to attract production funds. In a letter to the Ministry of Foreign Affairs proposing a rights deal worth 25,000 New Francs – an offer the Ministry duly declined – Philippe Lifchitz, Argos's co-founder, described the film as follows:

> *La Jetée* will no doubt be the first French science-fiction film. ... The poetry and ingenuity of its story make us hope for a totally original film worthy of the universally recognised talent of its director who, for the first time in his career, is abandoning all documentary and political preoccupations to concentrate solely on a '*Marienbad*-esque' essay.[20]

That Lifchitz thought it necessary to offer such reassurances can be explained by the fact that Marker's previous film, *¡Cuba Sí!*, a documentary sympathetic to the 1959 Cuban Revolution, had been banned by the French state. (The anti-colonialist documentary *Les Statues meurent aussi* had suffered a similar fate; though completed in 1953 it was only released in a truncated version in 1963.) Lifchitz's allusion to *L'Année dernière à Marienbad* (*Last Year at Marienbad*, 1961) can be read as the canny calculation of a producer: science fiction might not have been a staple of French cinema but the success of Resnais' puzzle-film proved that audiences had an appetite for works in which reality was served up as a riddle wrapped in an enigma.

Resnais was an important figure in Marker's life and work. The pair had first met in post-war Paris when both in their mid-twenties. Marker was working for the popular education organisation Travail et Culture and Resnais, he recalled, 'was in a cassock playing a priest in a Pirandello play'.[21] Discovering a shared interest in cinema, art and cartoon-strips, they became friends, and Marker went on to collaborate on a number of Resnais' early films, co-directing *Les Statues meurent aussi* and assisting with the commentaries for *Nuit et brouillard* (*Night and Fog*, 1955) and *Toute la mémoire du monde* (*All the World's Memory*, 1956). They also discussed working together on a documentary about the atomic bomb, a project that would eventually mutate into Resnais' first fiction film, *Hiroshima, mon amour* (1959), made in collaboration with the writer Marguerite Duras. Marker might have been alluding to this project when he confided in 1962 that he would 'particularly like to make a film about atomic shelters', stating that he had been impressed by Ranald MacDougall's doomsday movie *The World, The Flesh and The Devil* (1959).[22] By this time, he was preparing *La Jetée* and in January 1962 had written to Jacques Ledoux at the Belgian Film Archive, requesting that he screen for him a selection of recent science-fiction films with an end-of-the-world theme.[23]

Resnais was also one of the few people to have seen Marker's earliest experiments in film-making and he referred to them when discussing *La Jetée* in a 1963 interview. 'Its story relates back to the first films Marker made in 8mm in 1946', Resnais observed. 'I found the material [in *La Jetée*] to be much more polished artistically but identical in terms of the images and commentary.'[24] In an interview Resnais gave over thirty years later, he recalled the title of one of these early films as well as some of its salient features:

> I have this memory of the first film he showed me at his house in Ville d'Avray, which, if I'm not mistaken, was called *La Fin du monde vue par l'ange Gabriel* (*The End of the World as Seen by the Angel Gabriel*). It was a succession of images that weren't always identifiable and he was intentionally using a lot of out of focus shots and things like that, but the commentary was fascinating and I remember being really thrilled by the film.[25]

Marker never spoke publicly about his early film experiments. However, in a letter to the British documentary film-maker John Burgan, whose 1998 essay film *Memory of Berlin* he admired,

Marker confirmed some of the details that Resnais recalled, as well as adding to them. He wrote, '[Berlin] was the location of my first film (1947), [made] with a borrowed camera whose lens (but I discovered it only after my return) was regularly out of focus.'[26] Since his death, *La Fin du monde vue par l'ange Gabriel* has taken its place as Marker's 'official' first film in authoritative filmographies, such as the one compiled for the 2013 Centre Pompidou exhibition, which dates it as 'around 1950' and describes it as 'unfindable' (a subtle discrimination this and not quite the same as declaring it definitively 'lost').[27] The fact that the film remains 'unfindable' and has only ever been seen by Marker's closest circle of friends makes speculation about it irresistible and two lines of thought are worth pursuing in particular. The first relates to the context of Marker's early work. The second to a specific sequence of images in *La Jetée*.

La Fin du monde vue par l'ange Gabriel is an arresting title. With its combination of the apocalyptic and angelic, it condenses the images of earthly destruction and Christian symbolism that recur in Marker's post-war writing. In a detailed overview of Marker's early work published in 1963, the French critic Roger Tailleur described the poetry and fiction that he published between 1946 and 1949 as being written in a 'notably tense and tragic' mode, and these are indeed war-haunted works in which the frontier between life and death is paper-thin and the traffic goes in both directions.[28] One of these stories, 'Les vivants et les morts' ('The Living and the Dead'), opens with the Archangel Gabriel being chauffeured into an unnamed city under wartime occupation. Hiding his wings beneath his coat and tucking his halo, which he almost leaves on the backseat of the car, under his hat, the recording angel goes forth to meet a young resistance fighter named Vincent. 'How can I help you?' enquires Gabriel. 'To die', replies Vincent.[29]

'Les vivants et les morts' was published in *Esprit* in May 1946 under the name 'Chris Mayor', and its proximity to *La Fin du monde vue par l'ange Gabriel*, which was shot the following year, indicates that Marker was already working across different media and adapting his fiction to other formats. Another of his short stories, entitled 'Till the End of Time', which is dated October 1945 and was published in January 1947, was adapted for radio and broadcast in 1950.

Some of the imagery and narrative techniques in Marker's fiction found their way into *La Jetée*, which develops one of the central images in 'Les vivants et les morts'. At the beginning of the story, Gabriel meets Vincent in a garden 'filled with sad statues'. The occupying soldiers are described as 'recoiling before the striking sorrowfulness of these stone sentinels that remembered having been men'. And in the final sentence, Gabriel lays out Vincent's dead body, 'legs straight, arms crossed, like a statue on a tomb'.[30] Similar imagery recurs in *La Jetée*. From the setting of Chaillot, where the survivors shelter in long stone corridors peopled with enigmatic sculptures, to the images of defaced statues that 'ooze' in the mind of the time traveller, sculptures and statues appear throughout as mineral *memento mori*. It is as though a merciless element has flowed through everything – stone, flesh and film – freezing all in its wake: statues into attitudes of anguish; birds and animals into specimens under glass; man and woman into beings ambered by the lens. Time is this element, and it has deprived the film even of life's motive force – movement.

La Jetée is one of a number of films made in the post-war period where statues feature as emblems of mummification, of time moulded in stone. In Roberto Rossellini's *Viaggio in Italia* (*Voyage to Italy*, 1954), Resnais' *Hiroshima, mon amour* and *L'Année dernière à Marienbad* and Jean-Luc Godard's *Le Mépris* (*Contempt*, 1963), statues indeed have this symbolic function but, as Suzanne Liandrat-Guigues points out, they also stand in for the 'un-representable' war dead, the dead without tombs of Auschwitz and Hiroshima.[31] Statues are also part of a cluster of imagery, including museums and ruins, which acts as a 'mnemotechnic means' of connecting different temporalities, whereby the collective and individual times of History (with an overbearing capital 'H') and memory (with an inadequate little 'm') may resonate together.[32] This cluster appears in *La Jetée* among the images that 'ooze like confessions' on the tenth day of the experiments: an image of ruins, also mentioned in the narration; a museum, unseen, but described as 'perhaps that of his memory'; and four successive images of statues, which the narration does not mention directly. The sequencing of these statues and the transitions between them is significant. An image of the girl's smiling face prefaces the sequence that ends on the face of the time traveller, cross-faded with an image of a blank-eyed, sculpted stone head. Across this short suite of images of three sculpted female forms there is a visual association of sightless eyes and eroded stone bodies, alternately faceless and headless, the third of which writhes in a posture of love or struggle in the arms of a similarly headless male figure. If this sequence prefigures the first meeting between the time traveller and the girl, it does so in a notably anguished register.

The opening of *La Jetée* also features its fair share of ruins in the sequence that imagines Paris being destroyed in World War III. This suite of fourteen images does not appear in the workbook where it is indicated only with the words 'Sequence B: Destruction Paris', and a technical note referring to 'photographs'. Most of the images in the sequence do indeed look like photographs and, while it's hard to tell where they might have been taken, they show destruction on a scale that can only have resulted from bomb damage during World War II. However, there are noticeable differences in the resolution and grain of the images: some have clearly been shot as 35mm photographic stills while others look like frame enlargements, possibly from 8mm film. Which brings me back to *La Fin du monde vue par l'ange Gabriel*. Marker's first film was shot in Berlin in 1947, so there's nothing especially far-fetched in speculating that it might include images of the ruined city. If we recall Resnais' comments about the film's resemblance to *La Jetée*, as well as taking into account that Marker draws here on diverse material from his own archive of fiction and photography, there's reason to suspect that in the opening of *La Jetée* are remnants of his first filmed apocalypse.

Mineral *memento mori* in the museum of memory

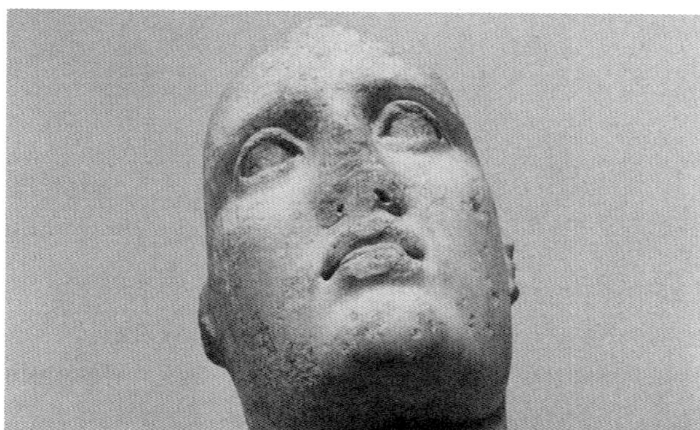

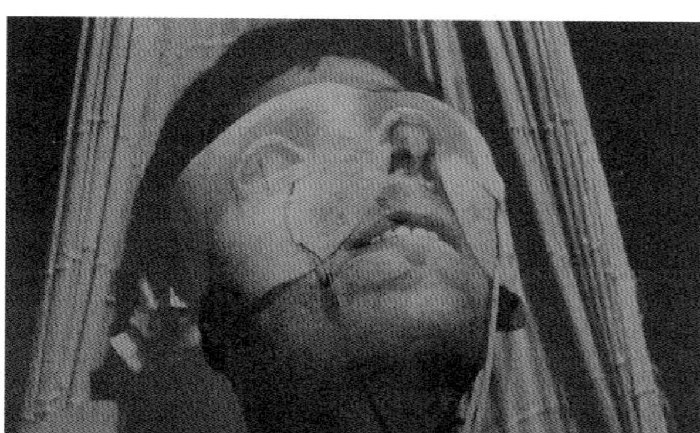

And then there's the blurred shot of a grounded aeroplane. As the final image of the opening scene at Orly that directly precedes the 'Destruction of Paris' sequence, it is no doubt out of focus to convey the violence of the scene in which a boy sees a man die. But might it also be – in the way that the *trouvaille* signals the *truquage* to come – a wink in the direction of the earlier, blurred images of *La Fin du monde vue par l'ange Gabriel*?

But it's not enough to see this sequence simply as an example of Marker-the-*bricoleur* rummaging through his archive to find images of destruction he didn't have the budget to film himself. Something else is going on. The images are organised in a precise montage, which takes us from panoramic shots of the Paris skyline to details of shattered streets and buildings. The final image of a decapitated triumphal arch is the only one in the sequence treated with a camera movement, an upward pan reframing the blasted entablature, whereas the transitions between all the other images are cross-fades. And while

The end of the world in Paris

this shot reasserts what the opening image of the Eiffel Tower under a flame-licked sky has already shown us – this is Paris at the end of the world – that is not all it does. Marker might have assembled this montage with words written almost 200 years before in mind:

> We fix our gaze upon the remains of a triumphal arch ... and we come back to ourselves. We anticipate the ravages of time and in our imagination we scatter across the earth the very buildings we inhabit. ... We alone survive from a nation that is no more.[33]

So, in 1767, Denis Diderot inaugurated 'the poetics of ruins' on which Marker's sequence plays its particular variation. The 'state of sweet melancholy' that Diderot described as the effect of viewing paintings of ruins is here reduced to a background note and replaced by a more traumatic register. After all, these are not picturesque, ivy-draped relics of antiquity, but ruins made within living memory on which a new world was being built. The emblematic structures of this new post-war world included Orly airport, which repeatedly features as an architectural signifier of modernity in French films of the period, ranging from Godard's *À bout de souffle* (*Breathless*, 1960) to Jacques Tati's *Playtime* (1967).

The three dimensions of time that Marker will conjugate throughout the film are there from the beginning: the present in the setting of Orly airport, the past in the images of World War II ruins and the future in a science-fiction story of World War III. The use of a science-fiction narrative as a framing device allows for the time-shift effect that *La Jetée* relies upon, whereby the present is seen as the past from the vantage point of the future. However, science fiction should be understood as only one component of the overall method Marker uses to organise his material, which here includes story elements from his earlier fiction, as well as photographic – and possibly filmic – documentary images from his own archive.

In his study of Marker's work, Arnaud Lambert examines the film-maker's approach to the image-as-document and finds in it 'a fundamental aspect of Marker's relation to images'. This can be summarised as involving three processes. First, Marker's recording of 'signs (and) material traces' of the world in photographic and filmic images. Second, his collecting of these images in an ever-expanding and constantly revisited personal archive. Lambert argues that this 'archival technique' is not one in which images simply satisfy 'a banal desire for embalming (reality)'. Rather, images, 'in "aging", break their silence, taking on different meanings each time'. A third process is needed for this to happen: images must be placed in new relationships with other images, which requires new films to be made and new forms to be developed to accommodate and reactivate the archival images, thereby also reminding the film-maker that, as Marker himself admitted, 'you never know what it is you're filming'.[34]

While one can imagine how these processes of recording, archiving and reactivating images informed Marker's approach to documentary film-making, how do they apply to *La Jetée*? In two ways. First, if images are conceived of as time capsules, full of the potential for surprise and revelation when placed in new juxtapositions or assembled in new forms – such as the photo-roman form of *La Jetée* – then this quality is crucial in a film where images themselves are the means of time travel. Second, it's worth noting that the Word War II ruins are by no means the only images of a documentary nature in the film. In fact, a great deal of *La Jetée* is made up of images that document Paris in 1962, including those of Orly airport and the Muséum Nationale d'Histoire Naturelle in the Jardin des Plantes. But unlike *Le Joli mai*, *La Jetée* is not in any sense a straightforward documentary about Paris. Rather, its documentary images are 'aged' artificially by being framed in a science-fiction narrative and, when seen from the perspective of an imagined future, these images of the present become those of the past.

3 Window Shopping in 1962

It makes sense to consider *La Jetée* and *Le Joli mai* alongside each other, both having been made in the same city at the same time. We might even think of *La Jetée* as a pendant work to *Le Joli mai*, a sci-fi supplement. After all, many of Marker's other major features were accompanied by works that were made concurrently, often in a different medium, and treat similar themes and subject matter. For example, *Le Fond de l'air est rouge* twins with *L'Ambassade* (*The Embassy*, 1973), a Super 8mm short about a fictional *coup d'état*; *Sans soleil* with *Le Dépays* (1982), a photo-essay on Japan; and *Level 5* (1997) with *Immemory*, an encyclopaedic memory-box of a CD-ROM.

Viewed now, over sixty years after it was made, *Le Joli mai* is a cinematic preserving jar that has pickled its time and place in black-and-white film. All the more so because of the way its 'direct cinema' style is as attentive to delightful peripheral details – like the spider bumbling across the lapel of a garrulous inventor who holds forth oblivious – as it is to big themes. *La Jetée*, on the other hand, has taken on the patina of timelessness becoming of a classic. Nevertheless, each film inhabits the other.

When I watch *La Jetée* I notice details from *Le Joli mai*: a stray graffito, a face seen in a car window, a young couple. The graffito is a barely decipherable slogan scrawled on the wall of a Paris street: '*Dieu existe la création de l'univers le prouve*' ('God exists the creation of the universe proves it'). In *Le Joli mai* it is shown full-frame immediately after an interview with a former priest turned union militant who explains the mutations of his faith. In *La Jetée*, it is one of the pieces of 'scribbling on the walls' that the time traveller and the girl use as their 'landmarks'. Among the time traveller's first visions of the girl is as a face smiling from a car

'God exists' graffito in *Le Joli mai* (1962) and *La Jetée*

window, an image that picks up from the closing sequence of *Le Joli mai* with its shots of pedestrians and drivers captured in reveries of inwardness while waiting for the lights to change. And then there's the couple themselves: a soldier and his girl. It might be going too far to suggest that these were stock characters in French cinema of the early 1960s, but *La Jetée*'s couple have much in common with other such pairings. Consider the real-life young couple interviewed in *Le Joli mai*, a soldier awaiting another tour of duty and his fiancée, totally self-absorbed in their love. And consider, too, *Cléo de 5 à 7* (*Cléo from 5 to 7*), the 1962 feature by Marker's friend Agnès Varda, in which the titular heroine, a young singer (Corinne Marchand), wanders through Paris anxiously awaiting the results of a cancer test. Among the people she meets is a young serviceman on leave (Antoine Bourseiller), whom she strolls with through the Parc Montsouris in a scene which shares some of the same sunlit romanticism of the walk in a Paris park that the time traveller and the girl take in *La Jetée* – the Edenic rapture of both scenes sharpened by the taint of death.

And when I watch *Le Joli mai*, I keep an eye on the background, looking out for a face in the crowd, hoping to spot *La Jetée*'s time traveller – *there*, gazing in wonder at a shop window, present in a past so full of promise for the future. A particular sequence in *La Jetée* makes an explicit link with the world of *Le Joli mai*. Twelve minutes into the film, on the thirtieth day of the first experiment, the time traveller meets the girl for the first time, but he's distracted by the things of 'this dateless world that first stuns him with its splendour'. Marker doesn't show these things but the narrator names them: 'around him only fabulous materials: glass, plastic, terry cloth'. Through a perfectly judged piece of temporal displacement, the signs of the future-as-now that *Le Joli mai* documents in displays of washing machines, televisions and cookers – not forgetting the exhibition of John Glenn's space capsule – become time-shifted in *La Jetée*'s uncanny image of the *future-as-then*. Suddenly, the time traveller is like an archaeologist, an opener of ancient tombs, who unearths a vanished civilisation's artefacts and is astonished by their modernity. The trouble is that, somewhere in another zone of time, other explorers are searching for the buried treasure that will let *them* access time's relativity – by excavating in his mind. And to emphasise this, the experimenters are heard whispering in German throughout this part of the sequence.

The idea that a man sent through time to save humanity should get waylaid by a spot of window shopping is a nice joke. Time travel with a dose of dry humour: the Marker touch. This is one of the moments when Davos Hanich is shown to have been an ideal piece of casting. A painter friend of Marker's, Hanich looks the part as a

A soldier and his girl in *Le Joli mai*, *La Jetée* and *Cléo de 5 à 7* (1962)

soldier in his thrown-together combat outfit, the sort who'd perhaps write poetry in his spare time. And given the evident limitations of the role – no movement or dialogue – he manages with aplomb to do the only thing left for him to do, to look like he's thinking. He also has another role to play, the one that the girl assigns him when she calls him 'her ghost'. But he's the most unusual of spirits, *a ghost from the future*, and as such his character suggests a way of thinking about how *Le Joli mai* and *La Jetée* inhabit each other: the future of one as haunted by the other's past.

Marker also uses the world of *Le Joli mai* to make the first of many allusions to Hitchcock's *Vertigo*. The time traveller recognises the girl and follows her, but is distracted by the fabulous trinkets on display and so loses her. In this short sequence there are various references to the scene twenty minutes into *Vertigo* where Scottie (James Stewart) follows Madeleine (Kim Novak) to the Podesta Baldocchi florist and spies on her through a mirrored door.

'Now he is sure she is the one': *Vertigo* (1958) via *La Jetée*, Paris 1962

Marker's scene recalls the setting and narrative of the one in Hitchcock: both take place in shops and involve a man following a woman, and they share the same visual details of ostentatious sprays of flowers and mirrors used to misdirect lines of sight.

The allusion may not be as direct as in the scene in the Jardin des Plantes – when Hanich indicates on the rings of an ancient sequoia tree where in time he comes from with the same gesture that Madeleine uses in *Vertigo* – but it's there nonetheless. Its function is to cue the first image in which Marker associates Chatelain with Madeleine. This follows directly after the time traveller's spot of

Hélène/Madeleine

window shopping, when 'time rolls back again' and 'the moment returns'. Having previously lost sight of the girl, now he is beside her. The profile shot of Chatelain, her hair pinned up in a spiral, is a direct echo of Madeleine when she pauses behind Scottie at Ernie's restaurant. In an essay on *Vertigo* published in 1994, Marker described this as 'the moment which decides everything' and to emphasise its significance in *La Jetée*, Trevor Duncan's musical theme rises on the soundtrack for the first time, its resemblance to Bernard Herrmann's *Vertigo* score adding a further layer of allusion.[35] The time traveller has stepped through the mirror into a world of 'impossible memory, insane memory' – the world of *Vertigo* as Marker describes it in *Sans soleil*.

In *Le Joli mai* Marker probes and praises Paris. In *La Jetée* he blows it up. Why? The obvious answer is out of fidelity to the times, to push the anxieties of the historical moment to their all too conceivable conclusion. Anxiety abounded as the dark backing to the period's increasing economic prosperity. The signing of the Évian Accords in March 1962 effectively ended France's colonial war in Algeria (ongoing since 1954) but the resulting peace was ambiguous and unsettled. Fears of nuclear catastrophe were heightened by the Cuban Missile Crisis in October 1962.[36] And the memory of World War II lingered. All of which informs *La Jetée*'s generalised sense of dread, its threnody for World War III.

A piece of correspondence held in the Argos archives casts an interesting light on the significance of war in *La Jetée*. In March 2003, an activist involved in running a pirate television station at an alter-globalisation forum in Florence contacted Marker requesting permission to screen *La Jetée* as part of protests against the looming Iraq war. Marker agreed, but made the following observation:

> [Even though] I've always thought it a misunderstanding to construe *La Jetée* as a film about war, its subject is something else altogether and the Third World War is only a backdrop … but no use troubling young brain cells with such quibbles.[37]

We don't have to take Marker's word for it but if we do we have to ask what, then, is the subject of *La Jetée*? Because the film is essentially a fable it invites and accommodates all manner of readings. It is perfectly understandable that Marker's reputation as a politically engaged film-maker has encouraged critics to interpret the film in relation to its historical moment. For instance, Jonathan Crary states that

> Clearly, *La Jetée* is not a story of the future but a meditation on the present, in this case the early 1960s, which Marker portrays as a dark time, shadowed by the death camps, the devastation of Hiroshima, and torture in Algeria.[38]

Catherine Lupton suggests that *La Jetée* 'forms the political unconscious of *Le Joli mai*'.[39] Carol Mavor dubs it 'a political fairy tale'.[40] Lupton's appeal to the unconscious and Mavor's to the fairy tale both qualify the film's political immediacy, and in doing so they touch on how the film frames its present moment, distancing and estranging it to reinhabit it anew from the perspective of the morning after the end of the world. This was a fashionable narrative mode at the time, as Frank Kermode observed of literary fiction of the period in *The Sense of an Ending* (1967), and Marker's apocalypse has the intention of making the present seem as fragile and poignant as the past. And if war is indeed only a 'backdrop', as Marker claimed, it is so in order that the foreground becomes the 'peace' that *Le Joli mai* documents as fact and *La Jetée* recalls as a memory.

There are two principal methods by which Marker distances the present: at the level of images and narrative point of view. As a documentary film-maker, Marker was intensely conscious of the way images 'age'. For instance, in the thirteenth minute of *Le Joli mai*, during a sequence filmed in the rue Mouffetard, as the camera pans over people in the street, the façades of buildings, and posters in shop windows, the voiceover commentary observes, 'Ten years on, these images will be more disorienting than those of *Paris 1900*.' The reference here is to Nicole Védrès' *Paris 1900* (1947), which was a key work in Marker's education as a film-maker, a compilation film about the Belle Époque made entirely from archive images filmed between 1900 and 1914. What in *Le Joli mai* is an observation about the perishability of images becomes the very project – or subject – of *La Jetée*: to artificially 'age' images of the present and to make them 'echo' as if they were images from the past. The method Marker uses in *La Jetée* to achieve this is that of a fictional war, not far removed from that employed by Védrès in *Paris 1900*, where the final images – free of commentary because they speak for themselves – show a trainload of soldiers waving happily on their way to the frontline of a real war. The purpose here, as Jacques Rancière observes of *Le Tombeau d'Alexandre*, is 'not to preserve memory but to create it'.[41] Or, as the narration of *La Jetée* puts it, 'Nothing tells memories from ordinary moments. Only afterwards do they claim remembrance on account of their scars.'

The last five minutes of *Le Joli mai* include one of Marker's most beautiful commentaries in which he likens the gaze the film brings to bear on Paris to that of a prisoner 'on his first day of freedom', or a Martian 'just landed on Planet Earth'. From the prisoner's perspective the question is 'how this strange phenomenon, free people, live'. Does their freedom and prosperity, experienced when they are 'perhaps opening the second great switchbox of human history since the discovery of fire', incline them to collectivity or to a sum of individual solitudes? The lyrical-dialectical thrust of the commentary condenses the film's principal subjects – imprisonment and freedom, despair and happiness, poverty and riches – to address ultimate existential fears. Over images of pedestrians and people framed in car windows, Marker's Martian wonders at the anxious expressions on these Parisian faces and asks of them:

> Is it the thought that your noblest deeds are mortal? Men have always known themselves to be mortal and have even found new ways of dancing and singing mortality. Is it because beauty is mortal that to love another human being is to love also its passing?

La Jetée picks up where *Le Joli mai* ends, posing the same question. But instead of a prisoner, or a Martian, it is another alien outsider, a time-travelling soldier, who lands in the same city at the same time and falls in love – all over again – with a girl smiling from behind a car window.

4 Chris Marker Takes the Stairs

There is no doubt that *La Jetée* is a unique film but it's worth remembering that it is also a short film. As such, it was both the product and beneficiary of France's flourishing culture of short-film making, as well as its influential *ciné-club* circuit, and of other less institutionalised networks of science-fiction, *bande dessinée* (cartoon-strip) and animated film enthusiasts. All of which influenced its festival reception and the critical responses to its release.

The film's uniqueness was acknowledged in the prizes it won, which ranged from the prestigious to the peculiar. The Jean Vigo Prize, which Marker was awarded in 1963, was the French cinema Establishment's recognition of young, independently minded film-makers. The Giff-Wiff prize, on the other hand, came out of cultural left-field. It was the first award given by the 'Club des bandes dessinées' (The Strip Cartoon Club), which was founded in 1962 by critic Francis Lacassin and included Resnais as honorary president. The prize – named after an imaginary creature, half fish and half cat, which appeared in the early twentieth-century American strip *The Katzenjammer Kids* – was awarded to *La Jetée* in recognition of the film's 'formal imagination, technical audacity and its contribution to the art of the strip-cartoon'.[42]

As for festival prizes, Marker turned down one and the other went missing. Marker's reasons for refusing the Golden Ducat awarded by the 1963 Mannheim Film Festival illustrate the vagaries of international film distribution in the early 1960s. A German spectator who had attended the festival wrote to Argos Films informing them that *La Jetée* had been screened three times, with the reels in the wrong order. The correspondent related that the reels were shown in a '1-3-2' order, so that the time-traveller's death took place in the middle of the film, while the end showed 'the tenth day of experiments, the thirtieth day with the meeting with the girl, etc., which constitutes the middle of Marker's film'.[43] This unfortunate remix was only part of the film's 'curious adventures' in German distribution. This was the phrase Marker used in a letter he wrote to the same distributor who had supplied the prints to the Mannheim Film Festival after learning that the film had also been 'reduced by half its running time "to facilitate its distribution" without either [Dauman] or I being informed'.[44]

However, consolation was forthcoming from elsewhere on the festival circuit. If the Giff-Wiff prize wasn't eccentric enough – though an award named after a half-cat half-fish hybrid seems fitting for a filmic photo-roman – there was the wonderfully named Golden Spaceship to set alongside it. This was the top prize of the Trieste International Science Fiction Film Festival, which *La Jetée* shared with the Czech feature *Ikarie XB-1* (1963). But when the trophy failed to materialise, Dauman had to pursue it on Marker's behalf until it was discovered tucked away in a Trieste cupboard.

July 1963 was the first edition of the festival. Reports gave the picture of a chaotic and impassioned event. The French director Pierre Kast described the fervour of interventions during a debate about science fiction as creating 'a climate like that of the wars of religion'.[45] Kast was a member of the festival jury, which had an interesting line-up, including French writer Jacques Bergier, Italian science-fiction author Luigi Berto, American film critic Gene Moskowitz, Italian literary critic Umberto Eco and British novelist Kingsley Amis. While Kast praised *La Jetée* as 'a pure diamond' and Marker's 'most beautiful film', Amis thought otherwise.[46] He concluded his report for the *Observer* as follows:

> The palm went to a piece of avant-garde kitsch, the title of which I will not advertise. It consisted entirely of stills. One of the Frenchmen, the one who kept saying we lived in a science-fiction world these days, explained that this severe self-limitation was excitingly experimental. Like having your leg broken before running a mile, I wish I'd thought of saying.[47]

In March 1966, when *La Jetée* opened in London in a double bill with Jean-Luc Godard's *Alphaville* (1965), the *Daily Mail*'s reviewer ran with Amis's ambulatory metaphor: 'It is all cleverly done, but to do it the hard way like this seems about as logical as trudging up a long flight of stairs when there is a lift waiting to carry you.'[48] This catches the tone of the British critical response to the film: respectful but underwhelmed. Reading the reviews, one hardly gets the sense of a work that would become an enduring cinematic totem. Rather, bemusement was expressed at the formal challenge of the film, such as in the *Financial Times*' assessment of it as 'a curiosity … it remains, in a way Marker's earlier films have never been, an exercise'.[49] Or the film's form was judged inadequate to its content, as in the *Observer*'s judgement of it as 'a clever montage that never matches up to the horror of its subject: nuclear war. Beside *The War Game* it looks too much like art: which means it is not artistic enough.'[50]

Others found more to praise. Richard Roud declared it an 'extraordinary short film' and noted perceptively that 'its subject – a fable of the future – is rather difficult to write about, not so much because it is obscure but mostly because it can really only be told in the way Marker has chosen to tell it: on film'.[51]

It took two authors of speculative fiction to capture why the film would have a lasting impact. J. G. Ballard contributed a piece to the British science-fiction magazine *New Worlds* that is as much an inspired description as it is a review. The film, he wrote, is 'a series of bizarre images of the inner landscapes of time'. Chatelain's awakening is 'a moment of extraordinary poignancy, like a fragment of a child's dream'. And the sequence in which the time traveller returns to pre-war Paris, 'the most remarkable in the film, the subject lying in a hammock in the underground corridor as if waiting for an inward sun to rise'. Ballard's conclusion is equally striking: 'Not once does it make use of the time honoured conventions of traditional science fiction. Creating its own conventions from scratch, it triumphantly succeeds where science fiction invariably fails.'[52] It is a claim worth reconsidering now that the conventions of

La Jetée have become the blueprint for any number of time-travel films where a boysy attraction to narrative gadgetry often overwhelms the emotional force of the original.

Like Ballard, the American film critic Ernest Callenbach, author of the Green-futurist novel *Ecotopia* (1975) and founder of *Film Quarterly*, plainly got *La Jetée*. 'I cannot escape the feeling that *La Jetée* is a great film, and will last', he admitted. 'It is a film of heart-breaking nostalgia – nostalgia for the ordinary life, the ordinary loves of our present.' Callenbach even appears to have discussed the film with Marker himself: 'Asked why he dealt so cursorily with the future, Marker does not seem to think this is a sensible question. He is not really interested in that; it is not a science-fiction film.' Callenbach sees the science-fiction aspect as novel but not the film's essential core. 'The overwhelming point of *La Jetée* is the simple, awesome difference between being alive and being dead.' And he too makes a critical judgement that needs reassessing given the time that's passed. 'There is no romanticism in Marker's portrait – no pretty views, no youthful zooming around Paris', he claims. 'The hero is preoccupied a good deal of the time; the girl is quiet, meditative. They do not really "do" anything; they are just alive.' It is arguably the very 'romanticism' of the film's views of 1960s Paris that now endows *La Jetée* with even greater pathos than on its release, and that endures despite the film's time-travel narrative being repeatedly rehashed by other film-makers with ever-diminishing returns.[53]

In France, *La Jetée* screened at the important Tours International Festival of Short Films in 1963 and was well received. The correspondent for the *France-Observateur* news magazine claimed it 'incontestably deserved the top prize', though it came away ungarlanded.[54] *Le Monde* described it 'as the most striking and perhaps the most original' film shown at the festival and claimed that, having won the Jean Vigo Prize for short films in the same year, it was out of the running for an award at Tours.[55] When the film was released in April 1964, it was as part of a carefully selected programme of shorts that opened at La Pagode, a key Paris art cinema. Argos distributed this feature-length package under the rather uninspiring title 'Un Cinéma différent' ('A Different Cinema') which, while hardly likely to set cinephile hearts racing, at least prepared audiences for a varied bill of fare. This included *Corps profond* (*In the Depths of the Human Body*, 1960), a scientific documentary charting the journey of an endoscopic camera through a human body; *La Cinémathèque française* (1962), a portrait of the fabled institution and its founder, Henri Langlois; *Igra* (*The Game*, 1962), a thirteen-minute experimental animation by Oscar-winning Yugoslavian animator Dušan Vukotić; and … *A Valparaíso* (*Valparaiso*, 1962), Joris Ivens's dazzling thirty-seven-minute travelogue about the Chilean port city for which Marker wrote the commentary. All in all, fascinating and esoteric company for *La Jetée*.

Crucial to the circulation of short films was the *ciné-club* circuit, the nationwide network of cinemas that both catered to and helped create the burgeoning cinephile culture of the time, which was served by specialist publications such as the monthly *Image et son*. Marker was firmly established on this circuit, and *Image et son* dedicated two special issues to his work in 1963. Its September–October edition focused on *La Jetée* and included a pedagogical dossier (the magazine was founded by a secular educational body), an analysis of the film and a version of the film's commentary. The interest of this document, published several months before the film's release, lies in the fact that the printed commentary differs from the definitive version and gives an insight into Marker's revision of it. There are three short passages that were subsequently cut. The first two relate to the early part of the film when the time traveller is introduced to the Chief Experimenter, who explains the trials he is about to undergo. They run as follows:

> Now the researchers were no longer concerned with the means of time travel. The war, which had made dreams of peacetime a matter of urgency, had hastened the experiments. To launch an object or a body into the past no longer presented any difficulties.

And then, following the lines describing how the time traveller was chosen for his fixation on an image from the past:

> This image had turned around on itself like an hourglass. Too many corpses had been seen during the war for the brutal revelation of death to preserve its violence, while the woman's face had come to be identified with the sweetness of life in a world without war, more irretrievable with each day. And when he pretended to let himself be carried away by the experiment they subjected him to, this man who had grown up in the war had the feeling that he was going to meet his first love.[56]

One can understand why Marker would remove these passages. They are unnecessarily expository but also, perhaps crucially, they repeat in words what must first and foremost be evident in images, and therefore *felt* by the viewer: the association of the woman's face with life and love during peacetime, which had already been established in the lingering shot of Chatelain on the pier at Orly. There is also an unusual narrative prolepsis here, in which the time traveller's feelings about the experiments are described before they have even begun. The other excised passage comes towards the end of the film when the time traveller, having fulfilled his mission, is transferred to another part of the camp: 'On the way, they let him breathe the air that his mission had successfully rid of its poisons. For the first time, he saw what the war had left of the surface of the world. Then it was back to the cell.'[57] Again, one can see why Marker cut these lines. By this point in the film, it's not the world outside that concerns the time traveller – or the viewer, for that matter – but the lost world of his childhood to which he longs to return.

A surprising feature of the countless commentaries that *La Jetée* has provoked over the years – and the film has proved a veritable machine for generating interpretation – is how little attention has been paid to its story, especially given Marker's reputation as a writer. It is to this that I will now turn.

5 This Is the Story …

With Marker, words came before images, writing before film-making. Thereafter a dizzying exchange takes place between word and image, page and screen, all the way to the 1998 CD-ROM *Immemory*, a representative hybrid object in his work but not the first. Over thirty-five years before, Marker had described *La Jetée* as a photo-roman, partly as a half-joking way of telling the viewer to expect the unexpected. By calling on an arrangement of words and images ancillary to cinema and closer to cartoon-strips, Marker lets us know that this is not a conventional film, and by folding the paraliterary format of the photo-roman into *La Jetée* – page into screen – he tells us that it will comprise principally of two elements: story and stills.

The photo-roman originated in Italy in the late 1940s. As Matilde Nardelli explains:

> *Fotoromanzi* were fictional photo-stories in cheap magazines, in a characteristic comic-strip layout [and] profoundly informed by cinema. In Italy and proximate countries, particularly France and Spain, their heyday, between the late 1940s and early 1960s, coincided with the heyday of cinema itself.[58]

Marker would have been alert to the photo-roman's distinctive arrangement of images and text, not only because of his enthusiasm for comic strips but also through his work for Éditions du Seuil where he was involved in the page layout and design of books. These included works published under his own name, such as the two-volume *Commentaires* and the photo-essay *Coréennes* (*Koreans*, 1959), as well as the series of travel guides he founded and directed between 1952 and 1958 under the title *Petite Planète*. These extensively illustrated paperbacks 'demonstrate Marker's sophisticated pairings of words and pictures', writes Isabel Stevens, 'with photographs used at varying sizes throughout: taking over spreads, jostling against blocks of text or colour, and arranged in lively sequences of small images'.[59]

In a 1957 interview Marker described typographic page design as a form of 'ersatz cinema'.[60] In his early films the back-and-forth exchange between page and screen is acknowledged repeatedly, such as in the first shots of *Dimanche à Pékin*, where an engraving of the entrance to Peking in a children's book dissolves into contemporary footage of the same scene. Or in the typewriter keystrokes that clatter over the opening credits of *Lettre de Sibérie*: the title bashed out in a typewritten font to emphasise the literary character of this filmic travelogue-essay. And at the beginning of *La Jetée* where, after the opening credits, two black screens featuring typewritten French text appear successively, which the English voiceover translates as follows:

> This is the story of a man marked by an image of his childhood.
>
> The violent scene which upset him and whose meaning he was to grasp only years later happened on the main pier of Orly, Paris airport, sometime before the outbreak of World War III.

As we read the words on screen they are spoken for us by a narrator who will remain a constant presence throughout the film. This doubling of reading and speaking is carried over into the narrative time of the story, as Janet Harbord notes: 'Whether the childhood voice of bedtime stories or the omnipresent voice of history, the narrator not only narrates the story but tells us that he is telling it.'[61] Harbord finds 'something of the fable in the narrator's address, the framing of the story precisely as a story in order that we understand there to be another layer of meaning'.[62] For Carol Mavor, *La Jetée* 'uses time in the spirit of the fairy tales of the Brothers Grimm and Charles Perrault'.[63] Whether we think of it as a fable, a fairy tale, or – why not? – a ghost story, *La Jetée* has the spare narrative elegance of these forms of storytelling. And while the earlier version of the

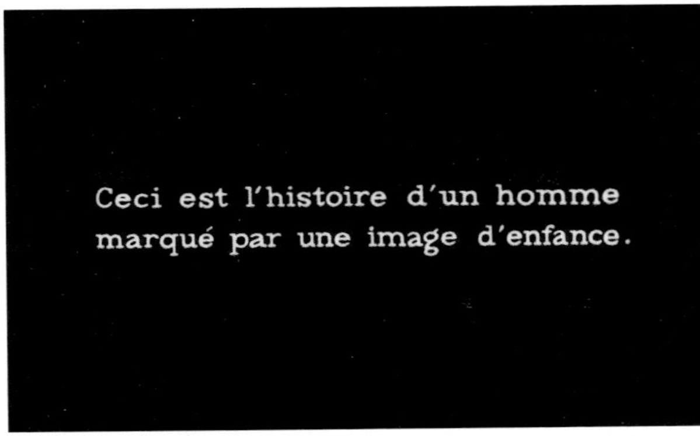

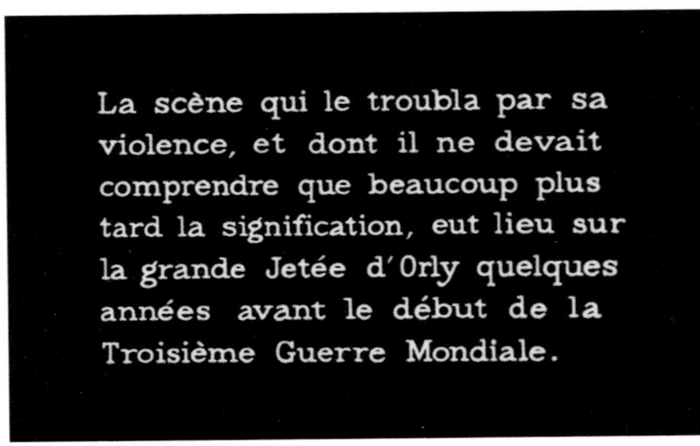

narration published in *Image et son* gives an idea of what Marker had to cut to achieve such concision, to identify the key motifs and narrative structures that shape the story we must look to his fiction.[64]

La Jetée was not the first time Marker had told 'the story of an image'. In the short stories and novel he published between 1946 and 1949 we encounter characters who are not simply 'marked' but *stunned* by images. The hallucinatory short story 'Till the End of Time' takes place on 'the day after VJ Day' during a torrential downpour, which shopkeeper Pat Cormon watches from inside his store. A demobbed soldier called Jerry stops by and, praising the A-Bomb, describes the end of the world to Pat as 'nothing like an explosion or a celestial fury. Something like, if you will … going rotten.' The apocalyptic tone is oddly small-scale, intimate and queasy, expressed through alimentary images suggesting digestion and expulsion. Against the background of a neon sign's 'great lickings of blue' and the rain 'hiccoughing' from a broken water pipe in the street, Pat's anxious mind fixates on what becomes the story's key image, the face of a woman who enters the shop, particularly her mouth – 'She had a beautiful face like a Northern warrior, and a violent, swollen mouth, shining in the rain' – and her lips and voice: 'The fascination of that mouth grips Pat … The Angel of Death calls with Her voice.' 'Till the End of Time' is the story of a close-up detail that threatens to swallow its main character whole.[65]

Elsewhere, Marker incorporates the techniques and terminology of film and photography, in keeping with the influence of literary modernism. For example, in 'Les vivants et les morts', the Angel Gabriel watches as the young resistance fighter Vincent takes part in an attack on occupying troops: 'What was this spectacle in slow-motion? … Gabriel didn't notice how the intensity of the scene had made him forget the rhythm of time. … Images followed one another without connection, like a rapidly flicked-through photo-album.'[66] But of all Marker's fiction, it is the novel *Le Coeur net* that has the most direct influence on *La Jetée*.

First published in France in 1949, and translated into English in 1951 as *The Forthright Spirit*, *Le Coeur net* is set in Indochina after an unspecified war and features an international cast of characters who have gravitated to a fledgling airline company delivering mail along perilous routes. The action takes place over several days and is narrated from the perspective of five principal characters: the Dutch head of the airline, Joris Van Helsen; the guard at a remote landing strip, Agyre; Van Helsen's journalist friend, Jerry Stone; the young English pilot, Kelso; and his lover, Hélène Marcheva.[67] The story is divided into two parts; the plot of the first part focuses on Kelso's treacherous flight through a heavy storm. When Kelso finally lands in the jungle he is shot by Agyre, who has been driven mad by hallucinations. In the second part, the lives of the characters are transformed by their memories of Kelso as he succumbs to death.

As a 1940s aviation novel *Le Coeur net* is of its time, fuelled by Saint-Exupéry's twin-prop metaphysics and piloted by Malraucian men-of-action-and-reflection. The adventures it describes are largely those of the characters' interior lives as evoked through their memories, dreams and reveries, which are conveyed in powerful sequences of images that inform *La Jetée*, as others have noted. In a key essay on the film the art critic Jean Louis Schefer says:

> I can't exactly decide whether it's a film or an outline for a novel ... the one who speaks in the film, he is not its author, but the author of the novel that the film blows apart, sketches out, jettisons, cuts, and whose substance it reworks.[68]

Schefer is a writer profoundly interested in images, time and memory – the same concerns at the heart of Marker's work – and he writes here as if he is perfectly aware of *Le Coeur net* but refuses to name it, as if making too direct a link with *La Jetée* risks instrumentalising the relationship, rendering it as banal as to suggest that the film were an adaptation of the novel. And while it is important to stress that *La Jetée* is not an adaptation, it nevertheless owes much to the novel. In the only essay I know of that compares the two works, Jean-Louis Leutrat writes:

> A book which opens with the image of an aeroplane taking off from the end of a runway and which concludes with the image of a woman alone 'on the edge of the landing stage', cannot but recall *La Jetée* – and as the separation in the novel is precisely that of death, then the connection is made insistent.[69]

Leutrat identifies key images and themes that novel and film share. I want to go further and suggest that it is in *Le Coeur net* that we discover how Marker manages the relationship between imagery and narrative in *La Jetée*. Take the novel's opening paragraph:

> An accident – it's nothing. It is quite literally nothing. There's the moment just before, when the aircraft leaves the runway, when a certain quality of silence, something static about the light all round it, seems to immobilise it, to make of it a petrifying fountain (so might a hurried angel strip a man of his soul a second before death, so is a bandage put over the eyes of a condemned man) – and the moment afterwards, when the aircraft is no more than a dart stuck in the earth, a burnt-out grasshopper, a crucifix. Between the two moments – nothing.[70]

Let us list the images that Marker uses to describe the plane crash. In the moment before: 'a petrifying fountain', 'a hurried angel' and 'a bandage put over the eyes of a condemned man'. In the moment after: 'a dart stuck in the earth', a burnt-out grasshopper' and 'a crucifix'. These images do more than just convey the action, they set the first links in a chain of imagery that will run throughout the novel. For instance, the 'crucifix' mentioned in the opening passage returns in the final word of the French text, '*crucifiés*', or 'the crucified' ('martyrs' in the English translation). They also decompose the action into a series of images, slowing it down, something emphasised by the words 'static', 'immobilise' and 'petrifying'. (The quality of the light around the accident is described as 'static' whereas the French phrase is '*certaine attente*', literally 'a certain waiting'). The resulting effect of narrative stasis is also a general feature of the novel, arising from the intensity of the characters' mental images.

And then there's that emphatic 'nothing', thrice repeated. Not quite nothing, then. The entire novel could be said to take place in the space of this 'nothing', between the take-off and landing of the plane piloted by Kelso. So, in the prefiguring circularity of the novel's opening, Kelso's death is foretold. This time 'between the two moments' – between flight and crash, life and death – also dictates the novel's two-part structure. We find similar structural ideas in *La Jetée*. The end of the film, like that of the novel, is in its beginning. And the time traveller, like Kelso, hangs parenthesised between life and death.

Film theorists have long tried to categorise the images in *La Jetée*, adopting terms like 'photogram', 'pictogram' and 'cinematogram', to characterise their hybrid state as somewhere between photography and film, stillness and movement.[71] But if we approach the film from the point of view of Marker's fiction – that's to say, as a story about images – another term presents itself. The images that surge forth in the mind of the time traveller appear, for us as for him, as *visions*. Broadly speaking, one of the things that images do in literary narration is to help the reader visualise the action and, while they indeed have this function in *Le Coeur net*, they are also frequently raised to the power of visions and, as such, it is they that become the action.

Three of the characters are more or less immobilised by the images that assail them. Agyre, stir-crazy in his isolated shack, imagines being trampled by hordes of angry elephants in a delirious vision that condenses the threat of the jungle around him and the storm that rages above. For most of the first part of the novel Kelso is lost in the skies. Flying off-course in heavy weather, fighting exhaustion, visited by visions of Hélène and memories of his violent childhood, it is as though he is piloting his mind through a storm of images. Meanwhile, asleep in her room, Hélène dreams of him. Towards the end of the first part of the novel there is a remarkable passage where the narrator takes us into her dreams and links the two characters in an extended visionary incantation on 'those two enchanted processes … love and death'.[72] The narrator tells her that it is the moments of love that will defeat death:

> When death tightens the thread and makes the final loop, it is through these memories that you will gauge your route … . Imagine that series of embraces, all tangled together as in those films where one movement dissolves into another … .[73]

The filmic simile here is highly reminiscent of the images in *La Jetée* that cross-fade in the time traveller's memory. And the image of Kelso flying blind finds a visual echo in the film's repeated shots of the time traveller lying in a hammock with his eyes masked.

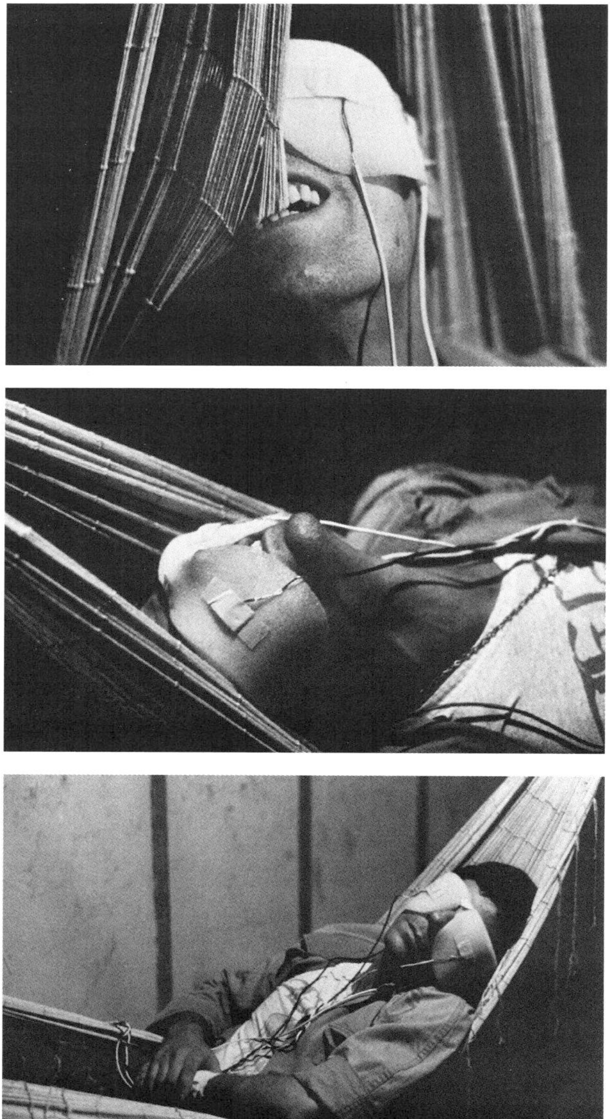

Visionary suspension

A *hammock*? What's this doing in a 'World War III underground concentration camp'? It's an odd little detail that we accept without thinking about. As an elegant solution to the problem of production design on a shoestring budget, it creates an image reminiscent of the shots of mutinous sailors in their hammocks from Eisenstein's *Bronenosets Potyomkin* (*Battleship Potemkin*, 1925). It also has an undeniably strong graphic presence, like a cross between a cradle and a curtain, obscuring the time traveller's face as he bites agonisingly into its taut folds. But this flimsy sling also carries a heavier weight than our time traveller alone because – like the sculptures and statues, the spiral of the girl's hairstyle and the sequoia tree – the hammock is a significant object, the meaning of which exceeds its obvious function. As *La Jetée*'s repeated image of suspension it is the emblem of the narrative technique the film shares with the novel.

The subordination of action to vision in *Le Coeur net* generates a sense of narrative stasis, an effect often produced by a character's experience of a moment of transcendent insight or piercing grace. In literary history, this mode of 'epiphanic' perception is seen to carry over from the Romantic poetry of Wordsworth into the modernist novels of Proust, Joyce and Woolf. In Marker's novel, however, we don't only experience this as the narrative condition that accompanies a character's epiphany, which Robert Langbaum calls 'lyrical stasis'.[74] And if we are to define the role of the visions in *Le Coeur net* and *La Jetée* we can say – following Chatelain's expression – that a vision is an image that 'echoes', expanding to fill the entire narrative space and arresting the action in the resonant stasis of *visionary suspension*. Just as *Le Coeur net* and *La Jetée* share this narrative mode of visionary suspension, so they also share characters – Kelso in his cockpit and the time traveller in his hammock – who can be described as *suspended visionaries*. To think of them in these terms allows us to place them in a lineage of similar characters, each one hovering in his own story assailed by visions, like acrobats hallucinating over a void.

Or like a cop hanging from a rooftop. For there is an influential reading of *Vertigo* that sees Scottie as one such 'suspended visionary' and the events in the film as his phantasmal projection. Charles Barr traces this interpretation back to Robin Wood's observation, made in 1965, that in the film's opening sequence Scottie is left grabbing onto a gutter for dear life with no way down: 'The effect is of having him, throughout the film, metaphorically suspended over a great abyss.'[75] In this account, everything that follows takes place in his imagination, which lends to the oneiric atmosphere of the film. Marker, in his 1994 essay, also subscribes to this interpretation of *Vertigo*, at least partially, arguing in favour of 'a phantasmagoric reading' of the second part of the film.[76]

While Marker was preparing *La Jetée*, a short film with a not dissimilar theme caused a stir. *La Rivière du hibou* (*An Occurrence at Owl Creek Bridge*, 1961), directed by Robert Enrico, was adapted from 'An Occurrence at Owl Creek Bridge', a short story published in 1890 by the American author Ambrose Bierce.[77] Set in the American Civil War, the story opens with a Southern planter and Confederate sympathiser named Peyton Farquhar being hanged from a bridge. Bierce narrates his fall, his extraordinary escape and subsequent flight back to his wife and family, only for it to be revealed at the end of the story that Farquhar is, in fact, hanging dead and these are the thoughts that flashed through his mind in the last moment of his life. Whether Marker saw the film or not, he would have been aware of the narrative device in Bierce's story through *Vertigo*. As Barr points out, the screenwriter Samuel Taylor explicitly co-credited Bierce in his revision of *Vertigo*'s screenplay, and Barr cites James F. Maxfield's claim that the film 'may best be regarded as an extended equivalent of Ambrose Bierce's story (and Robert Enrico's film) *An Occurrence at Owl Creek Bridge*'.[78] In Peyton Farquhar, Bierce created the prototype of the suspended visionary, whose subsequent incarnations include not only *Vertigo*'s Scottie but also the almost homonymously named Peter Carter (David Niven) in *A Matter of Life and Death* (1946) who, like Kelso, is a pilot hanging between existence and extinction. All of them dream the dreams of dying men. Like his fellow suspended visionaries, the time traveller dreams of love in the face of death – the 'two enchanted processes', as Marker calls them in *Le Coeur net* – and *La Jetée*'s circular narrative revolves around the cardinal 'image of childhood' that has 'marked' him, an image truly raised to the power of a vision – a woman's face.

Le Coeur net was a young man's novel, written when Marker was still in his twenties. *La Jetée* was a film made by a man in his early forties. That Marker chose to revisit the earlier work well over a decade later raises certain questions. Does the film come to supersede the novel as in the economy outlined in my first chapter, where later works displace earlier ones when their treatment of subject matter is deemed to be more fully achieved? And while we can take at face value the claim that *La Jetée* was a 'remake' of *Vertigo*, is this not also a classic piece of Marker misdirection, angling attention away from the *other* remake that the filmic photo-roman contains – the 'roman' being *Le Coeur net*?

There is no question that elements from the novel influence the film: the treatment of images as visions; the narrative mode of visionary suspension; the lead character as a suspended visionary; the recurring constellations of images of planes and faces. The 'tense and tragic' tone that Tailleur identified in Marker's post-war writing also suffuses the film, which develops the novel's key themes of love and death. In the final section of *Le Coeur net*, Van Helsen, Jerry and Hélène each consider Kelso's death. Among Hélène's anguished, uncomprehending thoughts about her dead lover we find the following lines: 'He had entered Death's kingdom without any markings, with no identity disc, no memory; she might pass him by, even touch him, without recognising him.'[79]

I have chosen this sentence as the epigraph for this book because it is a remarkable summary (or premonition) of the story that *La Jetée* tells, albeit with the roles reversed. In *La Jetée*, the time traveller enters Death's kingdom with his memory intact. The girl recognises him, and he her. He is even wearing a combat necklace,

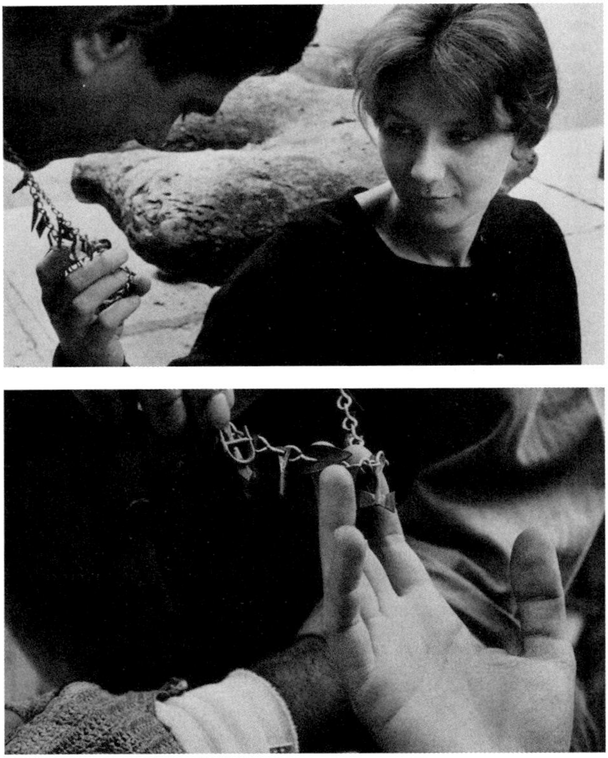

Identification in Death's kingdom

which the girl touches in one of the few moments of physical contact between the couple, a detail that recalls the identity disc mentioned above. But the crucial reversal that *La Jetée* engineers is that it is *she* who is already dead.

Not only is she dead, she is Death. We have seen how the image of a young woman's face strikes the fear of death into the haunted shopkeeper in 'Till the End of Time'. This image of death as a maiden is also present in *Le Coeur net*. The final section of the novel opens with a 'fragment of a letter' from Van Helsen to his friend Joel in which he writes about confronting death:

> But we belong to a generation that is used to early death. For centuries Death used to be represented by a broken, wrinkled old man, like Father Time. In our day it has come to be depicted as a beautiful young woman. A girl's death used to be as sensational as a crime; it would inspire the poets and the painters. Now when we look around us for images of death, they're all twenty years old.[80]

The girl so unforgettably incarnated by Hélène Chatelain in *La Jetée* carries over the image of death present in Marker's fiction. I suppose one shouldn't make too much of the fact that the character in *Le Coeur net* and the actress in *La Jetée* both share the name Hélène. Coincidence? That depends on your definition, so let's use Marker's own: 'Coincidences are the pen names of grace for those who wouldn't recognise it otherwise.'[81] And there's surely no point dwelling on the fact that this phrase appears in Marker's presentation of *Immemory*, where he muses on another coincidence of naming, shared by Proust and Hitchcock alike – Madeleine. He sums up his thoughts on the matter thus: 'I claim for the image the humility and powers of a madeleine.'[82] In *La Jetée*, Hélène is one such madeleine.

6 The Life and Death of Images

Let us begin with a thought experiment. Suppose that the version of *La Jetée* in which the time traveller is shown running along the pier was not simply a rejected cut of the film but one of a series of versions Marker had made, in each of which a different image moves, and that these found their way into cinematheques around the world. Imagine. An archivist in Buenos Aires rubbing his eyes when the 'real birds' really take flight. An audience in Tokyo thinking it must be dreaming as ripples radiate out from a boatman's oar across a glassy lake. A viewer in Helsinki convinced that the children in the park are a hallucination as they scamper pell-mell past the time traveller and the girl and out of the frame. But doesn't something like this happen anyway when we watch *La Jetée*? Isn't it implied by the blink of Hélène Chatelain's eyes, when everything that is arrested within the still image – time, movement, life – awakens? And so the possibility realised in this moment is released throughout the whole film in a chain reaction, its pockets of frozen time simply awaiting our imagination to thaw them back into life.

But the film defies the viewer's desire for the images to move. Nowhere is this better expressed than in the cruellest cut of the film, taking us directly from the 'awakening' scene to a shot of the Chief Experimenter gazing imperiously *straight at us* – we have become the time traveller and share his point of view – in a transition that illustrates the chilling line earlier in the narration: 'The camp police spied even on dreams.' And Marker toys with our desire. On the one hand, by filling his shots with things already stilled within the stills: statues and stuffed animals in glass cases. And on the other, by making these stills tremble on the verge of movement by suggesting their animation. Partly through music and sound – an aeroplane's roar, the time traveller's heartbeat, his captors'

whispered German – and also through cross-dissolves, fades to black and varied editing speeds.

La Jetée is an animation. That much is clear from the film's contract, the production credit for French TV's experimental animation laboratory, the Service de la Recherche, and the Giff-Wiff award for 'contribution to strip cartoons'. When he was in his seventies, Marker recounted two stories that reveal some of the film's secrets. One is about a cat, the other about a woman's face; both are meditations on childhood images that marked him. The first is also about an early experiment with animation. He tells the story of his youthful adventures in 'the unfathomable realm of Movieland' in an article from 1998. It concerns the Pathéorama, a handheld device manufactured in the 1920s for the domestic viewing of stills on a filmstrip, 'more like a slide show than a home cinema', by which one could view 'beautifully printed stills out of celebrated pictures'. Marker tells how, by devising his own filmstrip, he 'began to draw a few postures of my cat (who else?), with captions in between'. He showed his work to his friend Jonathan.

> I was rather pleased with the result, and I unrolled the adventures of the cat Riri, which I presented as 'my movie'. Jonathan managed to get me sobered up. 'Movies are supposed to move, stupid', he said. 'Nobody can do a movie with still images.' Thirty years passed. Then I made *La Jetée*.[83]

Before making *La Jetée*, Marker wrote about animation and incorporated its techniques into his films. In the early 1950s, he published four essays on animation.[84] Of the six films he made before *La Jetée* four contain animated sequences: *Les Statues meurent aussi*, *Dimanche à Pékin*, *Lettre de Sibérie* and *¡Cuba Sí!*.[85] There is a dialogue between these essays and films. Marker twice wrote about the animation studio United Productions of America (UPA) and paid homage to it in a parody television commercial in *Lettre de Sibérie* extolling the reindeer as 'the product to end all products'. Marker animated puppets, line drawings and also still images. In a sequence from *¡Cuba Sí!*, he crosscuts documentary footage of Fidel Castro in the Sierra Maestra mountains with animated stills of Errol Flynn in the Hollywood swashbuckler *The Adventures of Robin Hood* (1938) to lampoon the American media image of Castro as a Cuban Robin Hood.

One of the ways Marker suggests movement in *La Jetée* is through the editing transitions mentioned earlier, but another process was also involved in the film's production, which came after Marker had taken his photographs and before the editing. This involved working with skilled teams operating *banc-titre* technology. The *banc-titre* ('animation stand' or 'rostrum camera') was used to make animations, credit sequences, special effects and to reproduce written documents, drawings and photographs for films.[86] (The UPA-style parody commercial in *Lettre de Sibérie* includes a nod to Studio Arcady, the pre-eminent *banc-titre* team of the time, with Marker naming a pack of 'Horn Flakes' after it.) Having accrued the best part of a decade's experience with different forms of animation, Marker was familiar with *banc-titre* processes and *La Jetée*, being predominantly composed of still images, depends on them. (Though by incorporating a moving sequence into still images, Marker reverses the normal *banc-titre* process in which stills are incorporated into a moving sequence.) Along with the cross-fades, the *banc-titre* creates an additional sense of movement in a film where animation,

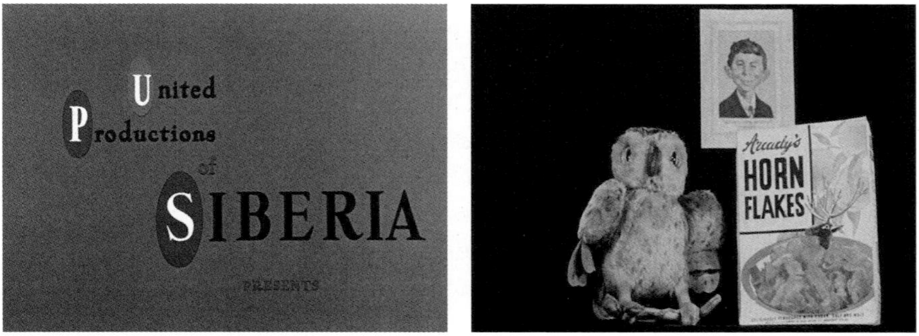

UPA-style parody commercial in *Lettre de Sibérie* (1957)

with one notable exception, is not so much about the movement *of* the images but rather *into*, *through* and *between* them. There are a number of moments where *banc-titre* effects serve to reframe images through movement. The opening pull-back along the observation pier at Orly replaces the moving shot of the time traveller running in the other version of the film. The pan up the destroyed triumphal arch is another instance of reframing for the purpose of emphasis, as is the short zoom into the time traveller's face on his first meeting with the girl. And his brief journey into the world of the future is economically evoked by zooms into a series of microscope photographs.

Marker was interested in how animation could introduce time to imagery and how this possibility appeared latent in images that predated cinema. In his essay on the aesthetics of cartoons he talks of 'this impatience, this straining of imagery towards movement that makes of the Bayeux Tapestry, for example, the unanimated drawing which ... lacks only time'.[87] Elsewhere, he pursues this idea in relation to Alain Resnais' films about art, stating that 'One of the fundamental powers of cinema [is] this gift of time which it alone can bestow on drawing, painting, or on imagery in general.'[88] However, *La Jetée* was not made of tapestry, paintings or drawings, but with photographic images, and therein lies the crucial difference. The former exist outside of cinema, whereas when Marker made *La Jetée* the photographic image was at the heart of the filmic medium that cinema then still was. In stripping cinema down to its basic element of the film frame and in appearing to remove the fundamental element of motion, Marker creates an interplay between stillness and movement that continues to fascinate scholars.[89]

Chatelain's 'awakening' comes, to put it mildly, as a surprise: movement animates the stills and cinema is born from a photo-roman. But it is a surprise that has been carefully prepared for from the moment, just over ten minutes into the film and on the tenth day of experiments, when images 'begin to ooze like confessions' in the time traveller's mind. The first six images in this sequence, and the narration accompanying them, are particularly significant.

As the poignant first stirring of the time traveller's memory, these images differ from those that have preceded them, and were drawn from Marker's own photo archive; like the 'Destruction of Paris' montage, they are missing from the shot breakdown in the workbook, implying they were not shot expressly for the film. But it is not the individual images that count so much as their relationship in a sequence, which is punctuated by repeated fades-to-black and emphasised by the recitative and enumerative narration. The narrator checks off the images like a shot-list, saying what we see. The qualifying words here are telling, as is the slippage from one to the other, from 'a *peacetime* bedroom' to 'a *real* bedroom'; then 'real children', 'real birds', 'real cats', 'real graves'. The repetition of 'real' gives the narration the feeling of a spell or a prayer, the word bringing the images into being. But what does 'real' really mean here? In his essay on Jean Cocteau's film *Orphée* (1950), Marker uses the same repetition to stress Cocteau's employment of cinematic realism in his poetic meditation on death: 'Heurtebise (a real chauffeur) entering Eurydice's home (a real young woman, inside a real house), to the sound of Gluck's *Orpheus and Eurydice* (real music, playing on a real radio)'.[90] Another clue appears in the 1966 re-edition of Marker's book about Jean Giraudoux, into which he inserted a new image to illustrate a passage dealing with the writer's valorisation of humble, everyday experience as the source of an ideal reconciliation between people and the world, whereby 'each thing rediscovers its Ideal face'.[91] Illustrating this phrase is an image of Hélène Chatelain from *La Jetée*, the same one as I have chosen for the frontispiece of this book. This brings us closer to Marker's use of the word 'real' in the 'peacetime morning' sequence. Here, 'real' means 'true' *and* 'ideal', in the sense that these images convey the Platonic 'child-ness' of children, the 'cat-ness' of cats, and so forth. As photographs, and as memories, these images represent both the particular (the one of a kind) and the ideal (the kind in its oneness).

The 'peacetime morning' sequence also has a specific structural purpose. It acts as a summary of what's to come, setting out the

The image as 'real' in the 'peacetime morning' sequence

key images the story will develop. The 'real' child is the emblem of the childhood the time traveller longs to return to. The 'real' birds and cats become the 'ageless animals' in glass cages he and the girl marvel at in the Natural History museum. The images of 'a peacetime morning' and 'a peacetime bedroom' merge in Chatelain's animated awakening sequence to the sound of 'real' birdsong. As a poetic digest, this sequence also condenses the life-to-death span of the film: from birth evoked by images of 'morning' and 'children' to the dying fall of the phrase – and images of – 'real graves'. It is one of a number of prefiguring moments – future echoes – that contribute to the story's circular narrative structure, as we have already seen in the '*trouvaille*' flash cut that prefigures the blink of Chatelain's eyes.

It lasts all of six seconds, this moment. Nineteen minutes (and forty-five seconds, precisely) into the film, we watch Chatelain waking. Her head on a pillow, her hand lying across her chest, she opens her eyes, blinks and smiles softly – straight at us. The impact

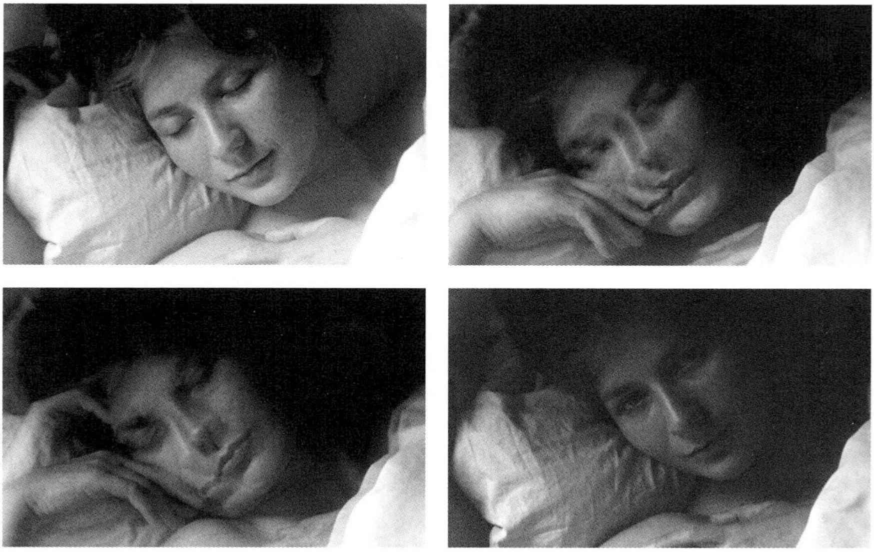

Awakening

of the moment is out of all proportion to its screen time because it manages to impress us with something of the wonder that the first audiences must have experienced at the birth of cinema. That the smallest of physical movements – a blink, a smile – should have such an effect is because – suddenly, astonishingly – they embody life itself. As well as being quite magical, it is also a moment of great tenderness imbued with a knowing eroticism. I can't think of a better illustration of Robert Bresson's famous line about 'the ejaculatory force of the eye'.[92]

This moment is prefigured partly by the 'peacetime morning' sequence and more directly on 'the thirtieth day', when the time traveller and the girl stroll through a Paris park. It is here, as she 'sleeps in the sun', that we witness her first awakening. Marker's brief but telling cross-fades on Chatelain's sleeping face rehearse the technique that will merge seamlessly with filmic movement later in the film. But even more significant is what is said in the narration: 'He knows that in this world where he has just landed again for a little while, in order to be sent back to her – she is dead.' A realisation all the more tragic in light of her later awakening, but also a reassertion of the twin poles of life and death that the film navigates between.

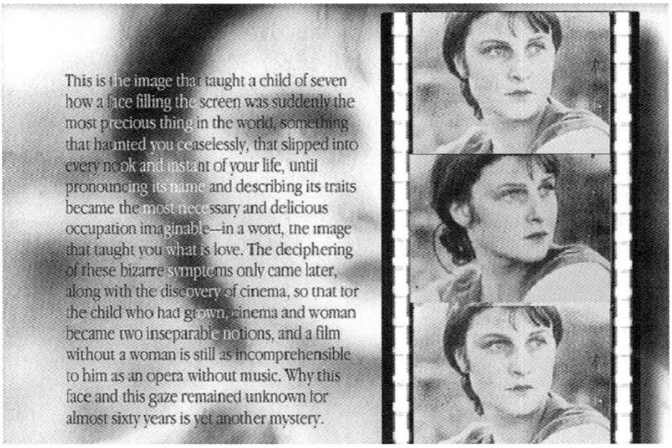

Simone Genevois in *Immemory* (1998)

Marker's work is full of faces: human and animal, sculpted and painted, photographed and filmed. But women's faces have a special place. He explains why in the second of the stories about childhood images that marked him, which features in the 'Cinema zone' of *Immemory*. Against a series of screens showing both still and moving images of the actress Simone Genevois in *La Merveilleuse Vie de Jeanne d'Arc* (*Saint Joan the Maid*, 1929), Marker recounts the following story:

> This is the image that taught a child of seven how a face filling the screen was suddenly the most precious thing in the world, something that haunted you ceaselessly, that slipped into every nook and instant of your life, until pronouncing its name and describing its traits became the most necessary and delicious occupation imaginable – in a word, the image that taught you what is love. The deciphering of these bizarre symptoms only came later, along with the discovery of cinema, so that for the child who had grown, cinema and woman became two inseparable notions and a film without a woman is still as incomprehensible to him as an opera without music.[93]

Marker's reminiscence continues across a further two screens in *Immemory*, but this captures its essence. In *La Jetée*'s images of Hélène Chatelain's awakening, then, Marker is not only paying tribute to the moment recalled above but also – and this is something far harder to achieve – re-creating it anew for those who come after him, allowing them to experience what he describes in the same text as 'one of life's most rare discoveries, the discovery of things that quicken the heart'.[94]

'Have you ever heard anything more stupid than what they teach in film school – *not* to look at the camera?' asks the female narrator in *Sans soleil*. These words could be taken as the motto of Marker's lifelong quest to capture moments of eye contact with whatever camera he had to hand. The most complete compendium of Marker's collection of looks and faces came in *Staring Back*, the retrospective exhibition of his photographic work held at the Wexner Center for the Arts in Ohio in 2007. The show's catalogue is itself a major late-Marker artefact and among its pages we find a face that stares back at us – and at *La Jetée*, too.

If, in Marker's personal mythology, the image of Simone Genevois lies beneath that of Hélène Chatelain in *La Jetée* – as the face behind the face – yet another face comes to superimpose itself shortly afterwards. *Staring Back* includes an image of the Russian actress Tatiana Samoilova, best known for her lead role in Mikhail Kalatozov's *Letyat zhuravli* (*The Cranes Are Flying*, 1957), which was among the photographs Marker had taken at the Soviet film studio Mosfilm in the late 1950s, and it had a second life in Marker's 1966 film, *Si j'avais quatre dromadaires* (*If I Had Four Dromedaries*).

One of Marker's lesser-known films, which was not shown theatrically in France until 1975, *Si j'avais quatre dromadaires* is a fascinating fifty-minute meditation on photography in which an amateur photographer and Marker-surrogate named Pierre muses in voiceover with two friends at the images he has brought back from ten years of travels in twenty-six countries.[95] A virtuoso piece of *banc-titre* work, it makes for a revealing companion piece to *La Jetée*. In fact, towards the end of the film there is a four-minute sequence that is little short of a mini-remake, beginning with the true story of a man who 'survived his own death' – a Hungarian soldier who faced a firing squad in 1956 and lived to tell the tale – and ending with a direct homage to Chatelain's 'awakening' scene, in which Samoilova takes Chatelain's role and a smile replaces a look. In between, Marker creates an atmospheric, allusive montage of stills that reprises key images in *La Jetée*: a museum, statues and sculptures, entwined stone bodies fighting off death with desire, women's faces. This sequence concludes with shots of Samoilova's face, rapidly cross-faded so that she appears to smile, thereby inverting the 'reverse smile' of the faces on funerary urns with which the sequence starts. To emphasise the reference to *La Jetée*, the last shot of the smiling Samoilova is cross-faded with an image of a bird in flight, repeating one of the key visual and auditory images of the earlier film, and to make the allusion crystal clear the shot that immediately follows is of Chatelain herself.

Tatiana Samoilova in Si *j'avais quatre dromadaires* (1966)

This sequence develops an idea set out at the beginning of *Si j'avais quatre dromadaires*, when Pierre discusses photographs of faces, and says:

> There is life and its double. A photograph belongs to the world of the double. That's where the trap lies. As you get closer to faces [in photos] you feel you're sharing the life and death of living faces. Not true. If you're sharing anything, it's the life and death of images.[96]

Marker's ideas in this film predate Susan Sontag's *On Photography*, first published in 1977 and in which she refers to *Si j'avais quatre dromadaires*, and Roland Barthes's *Camera Lucida*, first published in 1980.[97] Marker's film deserves a place alongside these canonical essays not only because of the elegance of its writing and thinking, but also because Marker was a photographer, especially of faces. As Johanne Villeneuve observes, the face in Marker's work is 'a matrix' – of meanings and allusions, of slippages from one face to another (such as from Genevois to Chatelain to Samoilova), and of different media (still photography and film).[98] But first and foremost, the face is a matrix of *looks*: that of the subject, of Marker's lens and of our own, and it is in the criss-crossing of these looks that the image 'lives and dies'. In this sense, *La Jetée* is the story of a man who travels into a time-tricked matrix of looks. He seeks the image of a beloved face, which comes back to life again as if it were a living face, and he dies under the eyes of the woman whose image has haunted him since childhood, the enigma of which, as Villeneuve points out, is *what she is looking at* when her image fixes itself in his mind.[99]

There is also death and its double. To return one last time to that room in the Whitechapel Gallery: there was another photograph from the *Staring Back* series that I didn't mention in my first chapter, which was the last image visitors saw as they left the room. It was a portrait of the head of a Chilean mummy: its features made alien by death, skin deeply leathered, head like a disinterred antique vessel, eyes sightless and oddly beseeching. To set it alongside photographs of women in their prime was to solicit a deliberate skull-beneath-the-skin frisson, and to suggest the idea proposed by Marker's mentor, André Bazin, of the photographic image as a technologically advanced form of mummification. Here was a being twice-embalmed, once in the flesh and once on film, looking from its wall back at *La Jetée*, in which animation defies the death present in every photograph. It was also there to close the circle on Marker's conception of images, which, raised to the power of visions, 'echo' and 'age', live and die. And to make of that room a shrine to the man who, among his many other achievements, refused to be photographed.

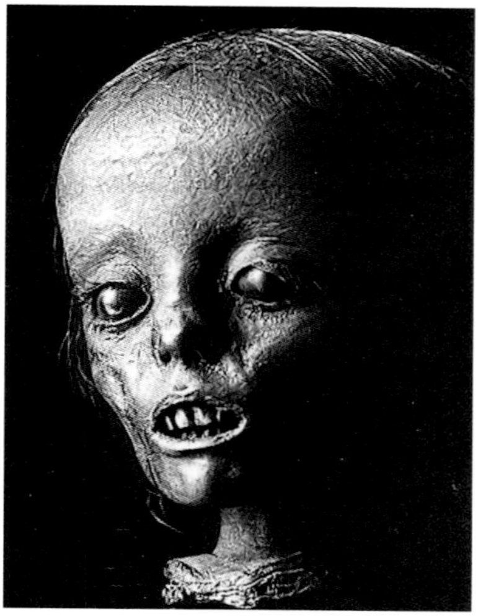

'Chilean Mummy' from the *Staring Back* photographic series (1952–2006, courtesy the Chris Marker Estate and Peter Blum Gallery, New York)

Afterword to the 2026 Edition

The fifth shot of *La Jetée*

There has been no shortage of tributes and homages paid to *La Jetée* since Marker's death in 2012; some predictable, others more unexpected. Who, for instance, would have foreseen an allusion to it featuring in the opening ceremony of the 2024 Paris Olympics? But there it was, in a filmed segment celebrating French cinema, brief but unmistakeable alongside quotations from the Lumière brothers and Georges Méliès. At the end of a pier stood a sober-suited figure sporting the same strange prosthetic spectacles as the assassin in *La Jetée*.[100] The homage made sense within a cinephilic frame of reference as well as in the context of the ceremony, for Marker's first full-length documentary, *Olympia 52*, was about the 1952 Summer Olympics in Helsinki, Finland.

Film-makers continue to cite *La Jetée* as an influence, though it could be suggested that they need the cachet of association to elevate their own work. A case in point is Asif Kapadia's 2024 docudrama *2073*, an ambitious if somewhat deadening experiment in what might be called 'doom-scrolling cinema'. The film employs copious news footage of contemporary horrors to foreshadow a fictional future where survivors of an unspecified apocalyptic 'Event' live amid surveillance-strafed ruins. Along with references to George Orwell's *Nineteen Eighty-Four* (1949) and Alfonso Cuarón's *Children of Men* (2006), *La Jetée*'s influence is present in visual quotations – the rings of an ancient tree marking historical dates – as well as in the film's underground setting and in the character of Ghost (Samantha Morton), a mute seer and gender-switched time-traveller surrogate.

It was inevitable that film-makers would submit *La Jetée* to the ordeal-by-algorithm of generative artificial intelligence, producing works that range from shot-by-shot 'remakes' to others where images from the film re-emerge in mangled forms that are deeply alienating.[101] Though Marker's alacrity in adopting media technologies is well known – he even developed a proto-chatbot called *Dialector* in 1988 – one wonders what he would have made of the terminally capitalistic nature of AI, with its hyper-extractive economy, ecologically ruinous impact and the rhetorical boosterism integral to it: *AI be praised! Finally, we have the technology to remove humans from their onerous responsibility of making art.* If such works are intended as a form of homage, to my mind they correspond to Marker's definition of the gesture as a disguised act of aggression. But the film can withstand such treatment. Perhaps its unhinged perfection even invites it.

Between 3 May and 29 July 2018, the Cinémathèque Française staged a landmark exhibition entitled *Chris Marker: 7 Lives of a Filmmaker*. It was an impressive show mounted on a grand scale and enriched by the inclusion of many previously unseen artefacts drawn from Marker's vast personal archive, which he had bequeathed to the Cinémathèque. Among the visitors was a middle-aged man named Jean-Henri Bertrand who, with his daughter Camille, watched a looped projection of *La Jetée* that was installed as part of the exhibition. Suddenly, Jean-Henri saw himself on screen. A little boy standing beside his mother and father on the viewing platform at Orly watching the planes take off. *There* – filmed from behind – in the fifth shot of *La Jetée*. Jean-Henri stayed rooted to his seat and waited for the film to loop round again. This time he was ready with his phone to snap the shot in question, which he posted to his family Facebook group with the words: 'Dad, mum and me in 62 at Orly, incredible. Seen in Chris Marker's *La Jetée*. Improbable but possible?'

Among the recipients of Jean-Henri's astonished message was his relative, the film-maker Dominique Cabrera. 'The vision of my cousin opened up like corridors in time', Cabrera said. 'There was a film to be made. A film which could be called "The Fifth Shot of *La Jetée*".' This was indeed the title of the documentary essay Cabrera finally released in 2025: *Le Cinquième plan de La Jetée*.

In the dossier she wrote about its making, Cabrera describes it as a film which follows the thread of 'a family and filmic investigation [with] its twists and dead ends, its moments of understanding and revelation'[102]. The thread that she follows starts with accepting the possibility that young Jean-Henri could indeed have featured in *La Jetée* and the little boy is her – and our – way into the world of Marker's film. 'To be in *La Jetée*,' she wonders in voiceover, 'is it not like being in stained glass at Notre Dame, on a frieze at the Parthenon, in one of Bruegel's fêtes? An anonymous face in a masterpiece for all eternity?' Her task is to reanimate that moment and to bring it alive in history.

One of the pleasures of Cabrera's approach is how she recasts a masterpiece into something else entirely: a family film. A productive and enjoyable tension emerges between her own quasi-obsessive relationship to *La Jetée* and her family members' reactions to her investigation. They're alternately engrossed and quizzical, playing along with her film-makerly immersion in the world of images. At one point, Jean-Henri's brother, Paul, a mathematician, stands at a whiteboard and calculates the statistical probability of Marker photographing the family group at Orly as a 'not negligible' 1-in-4,500 chance, adding that Jean-Henri seeing the film at the Cinémathèque was a 'much, much more unlikely event'.

Images are something of a Cabrera family business. We learn that her parents ran a photographic studio in the Algerian town of Sig before the country gained independence in 1962 and they returned with their children to France as 'pieds-noirs'. Her family features in her autobiographical films *Demain et encore demain, Journal 1995* (*Tomorrow and Again Tomorrow (Journal 1995)*, 1997) and *Grandir* (2013). *La Jetée* acts here, then, as a carrier of family and national-political history mediated by the images shot by Marker on the pier at Orly airport, as well as by photographs of her family and the clients of their studio. Cabrera returns to Orly to restage Marker's shot of the family trio. 'My life in France began here', she recalls of her childhood flight from Algeria. With a Pentax stills camera in hand (the same model Marker used for *La Jetée*) she says, 'I'm placing my footsteps in Chris's. A shamanic operation.'

Perhaps it's this shamanic aspect that allows Cabrera to break certain taboos attached to Marker – *Thou shalt not speak of me nor display any images!* We see carefully sourced film of him from February 1962, a straight-backed figure in a belted raincoat, shooting with a handheld 16mm camera at the demonstration against the Charonne metro station massacre at which nine people had died protesting the Algerian War. Marker's footage would appear in *Le Joli mai*, and among the faces in the crowd is that of a young woman, Natacha Michel, who became a writer and whose first novel, *Ici Commence* ('Here Begins', 1973), features a character modelled on Marker. Michel is one of the group of Marker's confidantes and collaborators whom Cabrera interviews, including Maroussia Vossen, Marker's adopted daughter; Catherine Belkhodja, his partner in later life; Pierre Grunstein, (uncredited) assistant on *La Jetée*; Pierre Lhomme; and Florence Delay, the writer and Academician who narrated the French version of *Sans soleil*. Cabrera gathers an unprecedented set of testimonies from those who knew Marker closely, the value of which has only increased since the subsequent deaths of Lhomme and Delay.

Or maybe it's because Cabrera also knew Marker herself that she felt so emboldened to talk about him. While some of her early documentaries were produced in the 1990s by ISKRA (the cooperative Marker co-founded with Inger Servolin in 1968, then named SLON), she had first met him when he was making *2084* (1984), a short film commissioned to celebrate the centenary of French trade unionism and to speculate on its future. Cabrera draws on *2084* for her film, which is likewise set in a darkened edit suite, the faces of people lit by the images on the monitors they huddle around, with the play of light and shadow illuminating their eyes and drawing attention to their voices. Along with the focus on family and friends, the film's *mise en scène* enhances its overall atmosphere of intimacy.

Cabrera understands that because her film is born of a chance encounter she is free to let chance guide her, something expressed in the Marker quotation she cites towards the end of the film: 'Chance has its intuitions that shouldn't be mistaken for coincidences.' It is around the enigmatic figure of Davos Hanich that this approach coheres to startling effect. If it is indeed the young Jean-Henri in *La Jetée*, she surmises, then he is, as Marker's narration puts it, 'the child whose story we are telling'. From this she extrapolates that 'he represents the hero of the film, Davos Hanich, as an infant. He is not only in *La Jetée* but he is at the heart of it.'[103] She advances the idea in the production dossier and in the film she pursues it to its limit.

Roughly halfway through the film there is an extended section focusing on Hanich. Cabrera screens *La Jetée* for his widow, Jacquie, and daughter, Lise, the latter having never seen the film before. Together they pore over Hanich's identity documents and it is revealed that his real name was David Bou Hanich, that he was Jewish and that he had been born in the same Algerian town as Cabrera's family, Saint-Denis-du-Sig. It's this remarkable coincidence that Cabrera takes as a pretext to explore something that she says she finds troubling, the resemblance between Hanich and the adult Jean-Henri. Jacquie and Lise are having none of it. 'Impossible', says Jacquie. 'It's nice to see a resemblance because we want to see it, and there's some kind of mystery', adds Lise. 'Like we've figured out something mysterious. That's a nice feeling, maybe that's it, what's driving you in this search.' But Cabrera persists and pursues the idea further with Jean-Henri and others in her family.

She has got to this point by way of a striking fact contained in an official document which she shows on screen: a list of people interned in Switzerland during World War II, which includes the names Bou Hanich, Davos and Bouche-Villeneuve, Christian. It's a vertiginous moment, one that calls for a freeze-frame and a voiceover saying something like 'Wait. *What*? Marker and Hanich were in the same World War II prison camp together? There's another film here, surely? One where Hanich perhaps plays a prisoner, based on Marker's experiences. A film that could be called ... *La Jetée*?'

Cabrera only brings this information up in passing, more interested in pursuing her investigation into the perceived likeness of Hanich and Jean-Henri, as well as their shared birthplace. But Marker's decision to cast Hanich now takes on an inescapable biographical and historical significance, and raises all sorts of questions. How did they come to be imprisoned in Switzerland? What was their time inside like? How did they get out? And what might this fact add to our knowledge and interpretation of the film? All questions that remain to be explored. *La Jetée* still retains its mystery.

Notes

1 Samuel Douhaire and Annick Rivoire, 'Marker Direct' (interview with Chris Marker), *Film Comment* vol. 39 no. 3, May–June 2003, p. 40. Translated by Dave Kehr. Originally published in French in *Libération*, 5 March 2003.
2 Umberto Eco, '*Casablanca*: Cult Movies and Intertextual Collage', in *Travels in Hyperreality: Essays* (London: Picador, 1987), p. 198. Translated by William Weaver.
3 Philippe Dubois, '*La Jetée* de Chris Marker ou le cinématogramme de la conscience', in Dubois (ed.), *Théorème 6: Recherches sur Chris Marker* (Paris: Presses Sorbonne Nouvelle, 2002), p. 15 note 14. All translations from French by Chris Darke except where indicated.
4 Undated letter from Marker to Dauman. Held at Argos Films.
5 *Planète Marker*, Centre Pompidou, Paris, 16 October–22 December 2013; *Chris Marker: Guillaume-en-Égypte*, List Visual Arts Center, Massachusetts Institute of Technology, Cambridge, Massachusetts, 18 October 2013–5 January 2014; *Chris Marker: A Grin Without a Cat*, Whitechapel Gallery, London, 16 April–22 June 2014.
6 Chris Marker, '*Marker mémoire* (Cinémathèque Française, 7 January–1 February, 1998)', in *Images documentaires* no. 31, 1998, p. 78.
7 Ibid.
8 See Chris Darke, 'At the Sign of the Black Cat', in Chris Darke and Habda Rashid (eds), *Chris Marker: A Grin Without a Cat* (London: Whitechapel Gallery, 2014), pp. 44–8.
9 'Hommage à Chris Marker', *Déjeuner sur l'herbe*, *France Culture*, 2 August 2012: radio interview between Olivier Kaeppelin and Hélène Chatelain, Nicole Brenez and Arnaud Lambert. The phrase Chatelain used was 'un veritable caverne d'amis, *La Jetée*'. Available at: <https://www.radiofrance.fr/franceculture/podcasts/dejeuner-sur-l-herbe/hommage-a-chris-marker-grand-entretien-avec-olivier-kaeppelin-8199746> (accessed 28 November 2025).
10 Ibid.
11 André Bazin, 'Bazin on Marker', *Film Comment* vol. 39 no. 4, July–August 2003, p. 44. Translated by Dave Kehr. Originally published in French in *France Observateur*, 30 October 1958.
12 Richard Roud, 'The Left Bank', *Sight and Sound* vol. 32 no. 1, Winter 1962–3, p. 27.
13 Ibid.
14 The contract states: 'Un film de science fiction tourné image par image et en noir et blanc'. *La Jetée* two-page contract, dated 19 February 1962, signed by Anatole Dauman and Chris Marker, p. 1. Held at Argos Films.
15 Douhaire and Rivoire, 'Marker Direct', p. 40.
16 Simone Dubreuilh, 'Flashes sur les jeunes réalisateurs françaises', *Les Lettres Françaises* no. 664, 28 March 1957, p. 6.
17 In Nora M. Alter, *Chris Marker* (Urbana and Chicago: University of Illinois Press, 2006), p. 130. Originally published as 'Chris Marker: Ich werde bestimmt wiederkommen' [I Certainly Will Return], *Deutsche Filmkunst* no. 1, 1962, pp. 26–7. Interviewer HH (name unknown). Translated by Alter.
18 See Philippe Langlois, 'Une pensée de l'image', in Martin Kaltenecker and

Karine Le Bail (eds), *Pierre Schaeffer: Les Constructions Impatientes* (Paris: CNRS Editions, 2012), pp. 179–89. The film's first television screening was on Friday 23 June 1965 at 9 pm on the second channel, which had started broadcasting in July the previous year.

19 Quoted in Arnaud Lambert, 'Image (Journey)', in Darke and Rashid, *Chris Marker*, p. 82. Translated by Trista Selous. Originally published in French in Chris Marker, *Giraudoux par lui-même* (Paris: Éditions du Seuil, 1951), pp. 25–6.

20 Letter from Philippe Lifchitz to Monsieur J. P. Campredon, Director of Cultural Relations, Ministry of Foreign Affairs, 18 October 1962. Held at Argos Films.

21 Jean-Louis Pays, 'Des humanistes agissants', *Miroir du cinéma* no. 2, May 1962, p. 5.

22 Francis Gendron, 'Le Socialisme dans la rue', in ibid., p. 12.

23 See Dubois, '*La Jetée*', pp. 18–19.

24 Guy Gauthier, 'Entretien avec Alain Resnais sur Chris Marker', *Trafic* no. 84, Winter 2012, pp. 55–8. Originally published in *Image et son* nos 161–2, April–May 1963. Resnais must have seen *La Jetée* shortly after it was completed because, according to the records of Argos Films, Jean Ravel had been hired in January 1963 for five weeks as 'chief editor', and the film's sound mix had been completed by early March.

25 From the transcript of an interview with Resnais by Birgit Kämper and Thomas Tode, 18 September 1995. Parts of this interview were published in German in Birgit Kämper and Thomas Tode (eds), *Chris Marker: Filmessayist*, vols 45–7 (Munich: Institut français de Munich/CICIM, 1997).

26 Chris Marker in a letter to John Burgan, dated October/November 1995.

27 'Chronological Filmography', in *Planète Marker: Le Guide* (Paris: Bibliothèque Centre Pompidou, 2014), p. 11.

28 Roger Tailleur, 'Markeriana: A Scarcely Critical Description of the Work of Chris Marker', *Rouge*, n.d. Available at: <www.rouge.com.au/11/marker.html> (accessed 28 November 2025). Translated by Adrian Martin and Grant Macdonald. Republished in extract in booklet accompanying *Chris Marker Collection* DVD (London: Soda Pictures, 2014), p. 22. Originally published in French in *Artsept* no. 1, January–March 1963.

29 Chris Marker (as 'Chris Mayor'), 'Les vivants et les morts', *Esprit* no. 122, May 1946, p. 771.

30 Ibid., pp. 769, 785.

31 Suzanne Liandrat-Guigues, *Cinéma et sculpture: un aspectde la modernité des années soixante* (Paris: L'Harmattan, 2002), p. 87.

32 Ibid., p. 86.

33 Denis Diderot, 'Salon of 1767', in *Selected Writings on Art and Literature* (London: Penguin, 1994), pp. 274–5. Translated by Geoffrey Bremner.

34 Arnaud Lambert, *Also Known as Chris Marker* (Cherbourg: Le Point du Jour, 2013), pp. 112–13.

35 Chris Marker, 'A Free Replay (Notes on *Vertigo*)', in John Boorman and Walter Donohue (eds), *Projections 4½* (London: Faber and Faber, 1995), p. 125. Originally published in French in *Positif* no. 400, June 1994, pp. 79–84. The Argos files hold an email from Marker, dated 2 February 2007, in which he emphasises the crucial role of Duncan's music. In response to a request for permission to remix the film's musical score in a live performance, which he refused, Marker wrote: '[*La Jetée*] possesses its own structural integrity in which all the elements, starting with the music, aim to create a single and unique emotion. And I stress the music: it is the exceptional quality of Trevor Duncan's that "fixes" the emotion, just as that of Bernard Herrmann (to which it is so close) "fixes" the emotion of *Vertigo*. Without it, there'd be no film.'

36 In April 1961, the French military had carried out nuclear weapons tests at Reggane in the Algerian Sahara, which was then still French territory. These tests included exposing soldiers to dangerous levels of radiation, details of which did not emerge in the French press until the late 1990s. Christophe Bataille's 2015 novel *L'expérience (The Experiment)* (Paris: Éditions Grasset) imagines the testimony of one of the soldiers used as guinea pigs and is influenced by *La Jetée*.

37 Chris Marker, email reply to Erik Lambert, 12 March 2003. Held at Argos Films.

38 Jonathan Crary, *24/7: Late Capitalism and the Ends of Sleep* (London: Verso, 2013), p. 91.

39 Catherine Lupton, *Chris Marker: Memories of the Future* (London: Reaktion, 2005), p. 88.

40 Carol Mavor, *Black and Blue: The Bruising Passion of Camera Lucida, La Jetée, Sans soleil, and Hiroshima mon amour* (Durham, NC, and London: Duke University Press, 2012), p. 60.

41 Jacques Rancière, 'Documentary Fiction: Marker and the Fiction of Memory', in *Film Fables* (Oxford: Berg, 2001), p. 157.

42 Francis Lacassin, '*La Jetée*', *Midi-minuit fantastique* no. 7, September 1963, pp. 67–8.

43 Letter from Heinz Steinberg to Argos Films, 23 October 1963. Held at Argos Films. (Letter in French.)

44 Letter from Chris Marker to Beta Films, Munich, 9 August 1963. Held at Argos Films.

45 Pierre Kast, 'Trieste', *Cahiers du cinéma* no. 149, November 1963, pp. 51–2.

46 Ibid.

47 Kingsley Amis, 'Spectacular Manifestation at Trieste', *Observer*, 11 August 1963, reprinted in *The Amis Collection: Selected Non-fiction 1954–1990* (London: Hutchinson, 1990), pp. 317–19.

48 Cecil Wilson, *Daily Mail*, 17 March 1966.

49 David Robinson, *Financial Times*, 18 March 1966.

50 Kenneth Tynan, *Observer*, 20 March 1966.

51 Richard Roud, *Guardian*, 25 March 1966.

52 J. G. Ballard, '*La Jetée*: Academy One', in *A User's Guide to the Millenium: Essays and Reviews* (London: HarperCollins, 1996), pp. 28–9. Originally published in *New Worlds* no. 164, July 1966, pp. 2–3.

53 Ernest Callenbach, '*La Jetée*', *Film Quarterly* vol. 19 no. 2, Winter 1965–6, pp. 50–2.

54 Robert Benayoun, *France-Observateur*, 5–11 December 1963, cited in *L'Avant-Scène Cinéma* no. 38, June 1964, p. 22.

55 Yvonne Baby, *Le Monde*, 4 December 1963, cited in ibid., p. 22.
56 Guy Gauthier, '*La Jetée*: Le commentaire', *Image et son* nos 165–6, September–October 1963, p. 104.
57 Ibid., p. 105.
58 Matilde Nardelli, 'Leafing through Cinema', in Steven Allen and Laura Hubner (eds), *Framing Film: Cinema and the Visual Arts* (Bristol: Intellect, 2012), p. 129.
59 Isabel Stevens, 'On Chris Marker's *Petite Planète*', *Aperture*, 24 December 2014. Available at: <http://www.aperture.org/blog/isabel-stevens-chris-markers-petite-planete> (accessed 28 November 2025).
60 Dubreuilh, 'Flashes sur les jeunes réalisateurs françaises', p. 6.
61 Janet Harbord, *Chris Marker: La Jetée* (London: Afterall, 2009), pp. 86–7.
62 Ibid.
63 Mavor, *Black and Blue*, p. 59.
64 Various critics have examined the influence of other writers on *La Jetée*. Michel Chion cites Jean Giraudoux's 1933 play *Intermezzo* and Adolfo Bioy Casares's 1940 novel *The Invention of Morel* (see Chion 2008). Raymond Bellour notes that the film shares the title of a 1930 short story by Henri Michaux (see Bellour 1997). Jean-Luc Alpigiano sees the film in the light of Jean Cayrol's 1950 essay *Lazare parmi nous* ('Lazarus Among Us') (see Alpigiano 1997).
65 Chris Marker, 'Till the End of Time', in Darke and Rashid, *Chris Marker*, pp. 117–23. Translated by Sophie Lewis. Originally published in French in *Esprit* no. 129, January 1947, pp. 145–51.
66 Marker (as 'Mayor'), 'Les vivants et les morts', p. 781.
67 In the original French version of the novel the English pilot is named 'Delso'. I refer to him throughout as 'Kelso', the name used in the English translation.
68 Jean Louis Schefer, 'On *La Jetée*', in Paul Smith (ed. and trans.), *The Enigmatic Body: Essays on the Arts by Jean Louis Schefer* (Cambridge: Cambridge University Press, 1995), p. 142. Originally published in French in Raymond Bellour, Catherine David and Christine Van Assche (eds), *Passages de l'image* (Paris: Éditions du Centre Pompidou, 1990), pp. 89–93.
69 Jean-Louis Leutrat, 'Le Coeur révélateur', *Trafic* no. 19, Summer 1996, p. 68. Bellour also comments on the influence of *Le Coeur net* on *La Jetée*, see Raymond Bellour, '*Marker Forever*', in Darke and Rashid, *Chris Marker*, pp. 70–4. Translated by Trista Selous. Originally published in French in *Trafic* no. 84, Winter 2012, pp. 15–21.
70 Chris Marker, *The Forthright Spirit* (London: Allan Wingate, 1951), p. 5. Translated by Robert Kee and Terence Kilmartin.
71 See Bellour 1990; Bensmaïa 1990; and Dubois 2002.
72 Marker, *The Forthright Spirit*, p. 106.
73 Ibid., p. 103.
74 Robert Langbaum, 'The Epiphanic Mode in Wordsworth and Modern Literature', in Wim Tigges (ed.), *Moments of Moment: Aspects of the Literary Epiphany* (Amsterdam: Rodopi, 1999), pp. 37–60.
75 Charles Barr, *Vertigo* (London: BFI, 2012), p. 46.
76 Marker, 'A Free Replay', p. 127.
77 A twenty-eight-minute, black-and-white film, *La Rivière du hibou* was one of

three shorts directed by Enrico based on stories by Bierce and assembled into a portmanteau feature, *Au coeur de la vie* (*In the Midst of Life*), released in 1964. *La Rivière du hibou* won prizes at the 1962 Cannes and Tours film festivals, as well as an Academy Award in 1964, and was screened as an episode of the American TV series *The Twilight Zone* (1959–64) in 1964.

78 Barr, *Vertigo*, p. 46.

79 Marker, *The Forthright Spirit*, p. 188.

80 Ibid., p. 181.

81 Chris Marker, 'Immemory', in *Immemory: A Cd-rom by Chris Marker* (Cambridge, MA: Exact Change, 2008), n.p.

82 Ibid.

83 Chris Marker, 'The Pathéorama', in booklet accompanying DVD edition of *La Jetée* and *Sans soleil* (New York: Criterion, 2007), pp. 17–18. Originally published in *Film Quarterly* vol. 52 no. 1, Autumn 1998.

84 See Chris Marker, 'L'Esthétique du dessin animé', *Esprit* no. 182, September 1951; '*Gerald Mc Boing Boing*', *Esprit* no. 185, December 1951; 'Une forme d'ornement (sur *Prince Bayaya* de Jiří Trnka)', *Cahiers du cinéma* no. 8, January 1952 (as 'Christian Marker'); and 'Cinéma d'animation: UPA', in André Bazin (ed.), *Cinéma 53 à travers le monde* (Paris: Éditions du Cerf, 1954).

85 Marker shared a director's credit on Walerian Borowczyk's animated short *Les Astronautes* (*The Astronauts*, 1959). He also edited Pierre Kast's *La Jetée*-inspired animated sci-fi love story *La Brûlure de mille soleils* (*The Heat of a Thousand Suns*, 1965).

86 A *banc-titre* consists of columns from which an animation camera adapted for frame-by-frame shooting is suspended. The camera can be moved along the column to produce a travelling shot towards the table where the documents or images are placed. To produce a pan the documents or images are moved on the surface of the table, which can slide from east to west or north to south, as well as being rotated.

87 Marker, 'L'Esthétique du dessin animé', p. 369.

88 Marker, 'Une forme d'ornement', p. 66.

89 See Karen Beckman and Jean Ma (eds), *Still Moving: Between Cinema and Photography* (Durham, NC, and London: Duke University Press, 2008); and Laurent Guido and Olivier Lugon (eds), *Between Still and Moving Images* (Barnet: John Libbey Publishing, 2012).

90 Chris Marker, '*Orphée*', in Darke and Rashid, *Chris Marker*, pp. 110–11. Translated by Sophie Lewis. Originally published in French in *Esprit* no. 173, November 1950.

91 Chris Marker, *Giraudoux par lui-même* (Paris: Éditions du Seuil, 1966), p. 45.

92 Robert Bresson, *Notes on the Cinematographer* (London: Quartet, 1986), p. 12. Translated by Jonathan Griffin. Originally published in French as *Notes sur le cinématographe* (Paris: Gallimard, 1975).

93 Chris Marker, 'Immemory', in *Immemory: Gutenberg Version* (Cambridge, MA: Exact Exhange, 2025), pp. 16–17. Translated by Brian Holmes. *Immemory* was originally conceived and published as a CD-ROM, first by the Centre Pompidou in 1998 and then by the US avant-garde publishing house Exact Change in 2002 and 2008. However, the subsequent obsolescence of its operating system rendered it unreadable. From thereafter until his death, Marker collaborated with Exact Change on a 'Gutenberg Version' of *Immemory* – its entire contents of words and images in the form of an English-language book and therefore more accessible than its defunct digital predecessor – which was finally published in 2025.

94 Ibid.

95 *La Jetée* and *Si j'avais quatre dromadaires* can be seen as part of a loose trio of 'photo-films', including *Le Souvenir d'un avenir* (*Remembrance of Things to Come*, 2001), which Marker co-directed with Yannick Bellon and comprises of photographs taken in the 1930s by Yannick's mother, Denise Bellon, a pioneering French photo-journalist.

96 *Si j'avais quatre dromadaires*, 1 minute and 55 seconds.

97 Susan Sontag, *On Photography* (London: Penguin, 2002), p. 5; Roland Barthes, *Camera Lucida: Reflections on Photography* (London: Vintage, 2000). Originally published in French as *La Chambre claire* (Paris: Éditions du Seuil, 1980).

98 Johanne Villeneuve, *Chris Marker: La Compagnie des images* (Dijon: Les Presses du réel, 2013), p. 94.

99 Ibid., p. 95.

100 See 'Full Opening Ceremony', YouTube, 26 July 2024 from 1 hour 23 minutes 47 seconds. Available at: <https://www.youtube.com/watch?v=onP5-DKSbI4> (accessed 28 November 2025).

101 See *AI Jetée* (Adrian Goycoolea, 2024) and Joanna Zylinska, *The Perception Machine: Our Photographic Future Between the Eye and AI* (Cambridge, MA: The MIT Press, 2023), pp. 123–46.

102 Dominique Cabrera, *Le Cinquième plan de La Jetée: Note d'intention et d'écriture*, press dossier, p. 3.

103 Ibid., p. 17.

104 Some published versions of the credits name Jean Chiabaud as Director of Photography. However, in an email written in 2007 to Argos Films, Marker clarified that Chiabaud's name was used only to satisfy the Centre nationale de la cinématographie (CNC), the state film body, which required that a film's dossier should include 'a director of photography with professional accreditation'. Marker goes on: 'So you will find in many films of that time names which are pure bluffs, credited only to neutralise the bureaucrats – which was the case with old Chiabaud (whom I nevertheless asked to film a wide shot of the jetty at Orly, of which I kept only a still image, that in the title sequence) who had to feature in the CNC dossier but certainly not in any technical credits.' Email from Chris Marker, 9 January 2007. Held at Argos Films.

Image credits

Lettre de Sibérie (Chris Marker, 1957), © Argos Films; *Immemory*, Musée National d'Art Moderne (1998); *Si j'avais quatre dromadaires* (Chris Marker, 1966), Association des Producteurs et Editeurs Cinématographiques/Norddeutscher Rundfunk.

Credits

La Jetée
France
1963

Directed by
Chris Marker
Screenplay by
Chris Marker
Director of Photography
Chris Marker[104]
Edited by
Jean Ravel
Narration read by
Jean Négroni (French)
William Klein (English)
Production Companies
Argos Films
Service de la Recherche de la RTF
Music
Trevor Duncan
Choir of the Saint Alexander Nevsky Cathedral
Special Effects Photography and Rostrum Camera
Jean-Pierre Sudre (microphotography)
DSA
Cs Olaf
Sound
SIMO
Antoine Bonfanti

CAST
Davos Hanich
Hélène Chatelain
Jacques Ledoux
André Heinrich
Jacques Branchu
Pierre Joffroy
Etienne Becker
Philbert von Lifchitz
Ligia Borowczyk
Janine Klein
Bill Klein
Germano Facetti

Production Details
35mm
1.66:1
Black and white
Mono
Running time:
28 minutes

Release Details
France theatrical release on 15 April 1964 by Argos Films
UK theatrical release in March 1966 by Contemporary Films

Select Bibliography

Alpigiano, Jean-Luc, 'Un film "lazaréen": *La Jetée*, Chris Marker (1962)', *Cinémathèque* no. 12, Autumn 1997.

Alter, Nora M., *Chris Marker* (Urbana and Chicago: University of Illinois Press, 2006).

Amis, Kingsley, *The Amis Collection: Selected Non-fiction 1954–1990* (London: Hutchinson, 1990).

'Around the World with Chris Marker, Part 1: Lost Horizons', *Film Comment* vol. 39 no. 3, May–June 2003.

'Around the World with Chris Marker, Part 2: Time Regained', *Film Comment* vol. 39 no. 4, July–August 2003.

Ballard, J. G., *A User's Guide to the Millennium: Essays and Reviews* (London: HarperCollins, 1996).

Barr, Charles, *Vertigo* (London: BFI, 2012).

Barthes, Roland, *Camera Lucida: Reflections on Photography* (London: Vintage, 2000).

Bataille, Christophe, *L'expérience* (Paris: Éditions Grasset, 2015).

Bellour, Raymond, 'The Film Stilled', *Camera Obscura* vol. 8 no. 3 (24), September 1990.

Bellour, Raymond, 'The Book, Back and Forth', in Laurent Roth and Raymond Bellour, *Qu'est-ce qu'une Madeleine? A propos du CD-ROM 'Immemory' de Chris Marker* (Paris: Yves Gevaert Éditeur and Centre Georges Pompidou, 1997).

Bensmaïa, Réda, 'From the Photogram to the Pictogram: On Chris Marker's *La Jetée*', *Camera Obscura* vol. 8 no. 3 (24), September 1990.

Bresson, Robert, *Notes on the Cinematographer* (London: Quartet, 1986).

Chion, Michel, '*La Jetée*', in *Le Complèxe de Cyrano: la langue parlée dans les films français* (Paris: Éditions Cahiers du cinéma, 2008).

Crary, Jonathan, *24/7: Late Capitalism and the Ends of Sleep* (London: Verso, 2013).

Darke, Chris and Habda Rashid (eds), *Chris Marker: A Grin Without a Cat* (London: Whitechapel Gallery, 2014).

Diderot, Denis, *Selected Writings on Art and Literature* (London: Penguin, 1994).

Dubois, Philippe, '*La Jetée* de Chris Marker ou le cinématogramme de la conscience', in Dubois (ed.), *Théorème 6: Recherches sur Chris Marker* (Paris: Presses Sorbonne Nouvelle, 2002).

Gauthier, Guy, 'Entretien avec Alain Resnais sur Chris Marker', *Trafic* no. 84, Winter 2012.

Harbord, Janet, *Chris Marker: La Jetée* (London: Afterall, 2009).

Horak, Jan-Christopher, *Making Images Move: Photographers and Avant-garde Cinema* (Washington, DC: Smithsonian Institute Press, 1997).

Kaltenecker, Martin and Karine Le Bail (eds), *Pierre Schaeffer: Les Constructions Impatientes* (Paris: CNRS Editions, 2012).

Lambert, Arnaud, *Also Known as Chris Marker* (Cherbourg: Le Point du Jour, 2013).

Langbaum, Robert, 'The Epiphanic Mode in Wordsworth and Modern Literature', in Wim Tigges (ed.), *Moments of Moment: Aspects of the Literary Epiphany* (Amsterdam: Rodopi, 1999).

Liandrat-Guigues, Suzanne, *Cinéma et sculpture: un aspect de la modernité des années soixante* (Paris: L'Harmattan, 2002).
Lupton, Catherine, *Chris Marker: Memories of the Future* (London: Reaktion, 2005).
Marker, Chris, (as 'Chris Mayor'), 'Les vivants et les morts', *Esprit* no. 122, May 1946.
Marker, Chris, 'Till the End of Time', in Chris Darke and Habda Rashid (eds), *Chris Marker: A Grin Without a Cat*. Originally published in French in *Esprit* no. 129, January 1947.
Marker, Chris, *Le Coeur net* (Paris: Le Club français du livre, 1950).
Marker, Chris, '*Orphée*', in Chris Darke and Habda Rashid (eds), *Chris Marker: A Grin Without a Cat*. Originally published in French in *Esprit* no. 173, November 1950.
Marker, Chris, *The Forthright Spirit* (London: Allan Wingate, 1951).
Marker, Chris, 'L'Esthétique du dessin animé', *Esprit* no. 182, September 1951.
Marker, Chris, '*Gerald Mc Boing Boing*', *Esprit* no. 185, December 1951.
Marker, Chris (as 'Christian Marker'), 'Une forme d'ornement (sur *Prince Bayaya* de Jiří Trnka)', *Cahiers du cinéma* no. 8, January 1952.
Marker, Chris, 'Cinéma d'animation: UPA', in André Bazin (ed.), *Cinéma 53 à travers le monde* (Paris: Éditions du Cerf, 1954).
Marker, Chris, *Giraudoux par lui-même* (Paris: Éditions du Seuil, 1966).
Marker, Chris, 'A Free Replay (Notes on *Vertigo*)', in John Boorman and Walter Donohue (eds), *Projections 4½* (London: Faber and Faber, 1995).
Marker, Chris, 'The Pathéorama', *Film Quarterly* vol. 52 no. 1, Autumn 1998.
Marker, Chris, *La Jetée: ciné-roman* (New York: Zone Books, 2008).
Marker, Chris, *Immemory: Gutenberg Version* (Cambridge, MA: Exact Change, 2025).
Mavor, Carol, *Black and Blue: The Bruising Passion of Camera Lucida, La Jetée, Sans soleil, and Hiroshima mon amour* (Durham, NC, and London: Duke University Press, 2012).
Nardelli, Matilde, 'Leafing through Cinema', in Steven Allen and Laura Hubner (eds), *Framing Film: Cinema and the Visual Arts* (Bristol: Intellect, 2012).
Rancière, Jacques, *Film Fables* (Oxford: Berg, 2001).
Schefer, Jean Louis, 'On *La Jetée*', in Paul Smith (ed. and trans.), *The Enigmatic Body: Essays on the Arts by Jean Louis Schefer* (Cambridge: Cambridge University Press, 1995).
Sontag, Susan, *On Photography* (London: Penguin, 2002).
Tailleur, Roger, 'Markeriana: A Scarcely Critical Description of the Work of Chris Marker', *Rouge*, n.d. Available at: <www.rouge.com.au/11/marker.html> (accessed 28 November 2025).
'The Owl's Legacy: In Memory of Chris Marker (1921–2012)', *Sight and Sound* vol. 22 no. 10, October 2012.
Villeneuve, Johanne, *Chris Marker: La Compagnie des images* (Dijon: Les Presses du réel, 2013).